THE LAST SCOT
1661 - 1714

by
Stuart Reid

Colour flags and uniforms by Stuart Reid & Jay Forster

PARTIZAN PRESS

First published in Great Britain 2003
by Partizan Press
816 - 818 London Road, Leigh-on-sea,
Essex, SS9 3NH
Ph/Fx: +44 (0) 1702 473986
Email: ask@caliverbooks.com
www.caliverbooks.com

Thousands of military history titles in stock!!!
Send 3x1st class stamps, 5 Euros or US$5 in bills
for catalogues. Please state periods of interest.

© Stuart Reid 2003

Stuart Reid has asserted his right under the
Copyright Designs and Patent Act 1988
to be identified as the author of this work

All rights reserved. No part of this book may be
reprinted or reproduced or utilised in any form or
by any electronic, mechanical or other means, now
known or hereafter invented, including
photocopying and recording, or in any information
storage or retrieval system, without the
permission in writing from the publishers.

ISBN: 1-85818-515-7

Design & Production (& colouring in!)
by Jay Forster (www.generate.me.uk)
Additional typesetting by Matt Hamm

Printed in the UK by Fairway Litho & Print,
Basildon, Essex

Partizan Historical series:
1 The Origin and Development of Military Tartans
 James D Scarlett
2 The Last Scots Army 1661-1714
 Stuart Reid

Coming soon
• Russian Opolchenie of the Napoleonic Wars
 Dr. Stephen Summerfield
• Cossack Hurrah!!: Russian Irregular Cavalry
 Organisation and Uniforms During the
 Napoleonic War
 Dr. Stephen Summerfield

Contents

THE LAST SCOTS ARMY
1661-1714

The British Army Traditionally traces its origins to that day on Tower Hill in 1660 when the last remaining regiments of what had once been the New Model Army symbolically laid down their arms as soldiers of the English Republic and then took them up again as soldiers of the Crown. They were still English soldiers of course and north of the border an entirely new army was coming into being which was to lead a quite independent existence for the next 45 years, before eventually joining with the English one to create the British Army.

At first this new Scots Army comprised only the traditional guards and garrisons charged with looking after Royal castles such as Edinburgh, but political unrest and a string of foreign wars compelled the recruitment of marching regiments which would see action against the Covenanters at Rullion Green in 1666 and Bothwell Bridge in 1679, in the Jacobite War of 1689-92, and afterwards abroad in Flanders under Dutch William and the great Duke of Marlborough.

Unlike earlier Scots armies it was recruited not through the old fencible system - which now became a substitute for a militia - but from volunteers enlisted by beat of drum to serve wherever and for so long as they were required - and for some of them that meant the service of France or Holland as well as Scotland. And instead of the traditional hodden grey of Scotland, they wore the King's red coat ...

Stuart Reid, 2003

UNIFORMS

For so long as Scotland enjoyed its political independence the Scots army also maintained a considerable independence from the larger English establishment. This independence is most readily seen in the uniforms worn by Scots soldiers and more particularly in the matter of "facings". Generally speaking contemporary English regiments wore red coats and were distinguished one from another by their "facing" colours - chosen by their several Colonels - that is the coloured linings prominently displayed on the heavy turned-back cuffs of the soldiers' coats. This practice of lining coats with a contrasting colour of material can be traced back to Elizabethan times and was extensively used by Parliamentarian regiments during the Civil War but there was no such tradition amongst Scottish units.

Red coats were adopted by the Scots standing forces raised after the Restoration but not coloured facings. The coats issued to Scots soldiers had, with certain exceptions discussed below, a plain white lining. This lack of coloured facings may be attributed in some part to the chronic inability of the Scots cloth trade to produce coloured material in sufficient quantity or quality. Despite a valiant attempt to do so the New Mills Cloth Manufactory was even incapable of producing sufficient red cloth to make the soldiers' coats and despite the proprietors' objections licences were given to several colonels to import red cloth from England for this purpose. No other colours of material were permitted to be imported and so strict were the Scots customs officers that even the cloth wrappings to the bales of material had to be comprised within the licences. In view of this parlous state of affairs it is perhaps little wonder that all but a handful of Scots regiments had plain white linings to their coats.

Both the Scots Guards and the Royal Regiment (Royal Scots) exchanged their white facings for blue at the Union of the Parliaments in 1707 but other than these there were only five exceptions to the general rule that Scots regiments in the period covered by this volume had white linings to their coats. The Royal Regiment of Scots Dragoons who, for many years, had worn stone grey coats adopted red coats with blue facings in 1685 but significantly they did so whilst serving in England. In the same year Colonel John Graham of Claverhouse's Regiment of Horse became the Royal Regiment of Horse and exchanged their white linings for King James' yellow livery. This was also the case with Colonel John Wauchope's Regiment of Foot, raised in 1688 by James VII largely to employ those officers of the Scots Brigade who had obeyed his order to return from Holland. The Earl of Argyle's regiment, raised in 1689, also wore red coats with yellow facings - and yellow stockings - again presumably deriving from his livery. He appears to have been prepared to spend a considerable amount of money on the clothing of his regiment and much of it, including presumably the yellow material for the facings was bought in England. The fifth regiment was the Scots Fusiliers. The first mention of their red facings appears to be in 1691 by which time they had been taken on to the English establishment so it was possible that in their earliest years they too had plain white linings. On the other hand the Fusiliers had their origin in a single company of foot raised in 1677 and ordered to be trained as grenadiers and "instructed in all things belonging to the artillery". This included gunnery so it might not be unreasonable to expect their uniform to have conformed to that of the artillery and there are indications that Scotland's gunners had red coats lined red.

Not all regiments, though, had red coats. Sir William Lockhart's Foot levied in 1672 had blue coats lined white. The choice of blue, in this case being accounted for by the fact that the regiment was raised not by beat of drum but instead by conscripting fencibles. The levying instructions clearly imply that they were in fact wearing militia uniform. The Royal Regiment of Scots Dragoons, of course, wore stone grey coats instead of red in their early years at the insistence of General Dalyell. A third exception was the Earl of Lindsay's Regiment of Foot raised in 1694 which had coats of white Galloway cloth. Since no mention is made of coloured facings in the otherwise detailed lists of clothing for the unit it may not unreasonably be concluded that they also had white linings. Why they should have been clothed thus is not explained, but it may have come down to simple economics.

The coats themselves were knee-length, generally buttoned from neck to hem with tin or brass buttons (usually the former), with large turned back cuffs. As a rule serge was used for linings although harden - a coarse linen - is often mentioned. After the Revolution the coats were frequently referred to as *Piecoats* a curious term which is evidently a corruption of the Dutch word *Pij* meaning a frock or habit, in other words a frock-coat (it has since further been corrupted into *Pea* as in Pea-jacket). This may simply reflect the adoption of Dutch slang but more likely indicates a coat with a tailored waist introduced to suit the wearing of a waistbelt to accommodate the bayonet. Earlier coats were hung from the shoulders with no defined waist. About two English ells went into each coat.

Grenadiers were distinguished not only by their headgear and equipment, but in some cases by their "looped clothes" - their coats being decorated with loops of white worsted tape at the buttonholes, sometimes tufted at the ends and frequently having a coloured thread worked into the tape as a regimental distinction. This was certainly the case with regiments on the English establishment such as the Royal Regiment (Royal Scots) but evidence is lacking as to how widespread it might have been amongst units on the Scots establishment.

During the reign of Charles II the Scots Guards and the Royal regiment had white scarves for the pikemen but the practice appears to have died out under James VII. Officers and sergeants were distinguished by the wearing of a crimson scarf; like the pikemen both at first wore it tied sash-wise around the waist but by the time of Queen Anne, while sergeants continued to wear it thus, officers had for the most part transferred theirs to the shoulder.

Under their red coats soldiers wore a sleeved waistcoat. These were not actually issued to them and so presumably, as in the 18th C., they were made from the previous year's red coats.

Only sufficient red cloth for coats could be imported and the native article was in consequence used for knee breeches. Why therefore the Scots Fusiliers were known as "The Earl O' Mar's Greybreeks" is not entirely clear since at the time most soldiers on the Scots establishment had grey breeches. The Scots Guards had white breeches and stockings but the Royal Regiment too had grey. Breeches were, it seems, rather low down on the scale of priorities and in some instances it is clear that soldiers were issued with no clothing except a hat and coat (and sometimes not even a hat). In such cases the soldiers will have been wearing very largely their own clothes and hodden grey will have predominated. Officers in any case always seem to have dressed as they pleased. Sergeants in the Earl of Lindsay's Regiment received red breeches in 1694 and this privilege may well have been extended to sergeants of other units.

Stockings too were generally grey although the Guards had white ones, Argyle's had yellow and Lindsay's red.

The question of the style of headgear worn by Scots regiments in the second half of the 17th C. is most interesting. The standing forces for the most part had black broad-brimmed hats, bound around with white or yellow tape (depending on whether tin or brass buttons appeared on their coats). The Scots Guards, the Royal Regiment, Lockhart's Foot, Wauchope's and the Earl of Angus's certainly did, to name but a few and even the militia seem in many cases to have had them. Some units, however, clung to the old Scots blew cap or bonnet. The Grey Dragoons certainly did so and some militia units likewise, especially in the early days, although this probably reflects a lack of hats being issued rather than an issue of bonnets. The Earl of Argyle's Regiment was certainly issued with bonnets, with a boar's head crest and coronet embroidered thereon and the Laird of Grant's Regiment raised in the same year probably had bonnets also since a petition mentions the provision of coats, muskets and accoutrements but makes no mention of headgear. In 1694 the Earl of Lindsay's Regiment was issued with caps. Lawson interpreted these as being fusilier type ones but while the wearing of fusilier caps was becoming common enough amongst regiments in Flanders for King William to forbid the practice there is some reason to believe that the caps issued to Lindsay's Regiment may have been bonnets.

Grenadier caps were another aspect of the Scots army's sartorial independence. English grenadiers on their first being formed in 1677 wore furred caps but by the beginning of the 1680s these had given way to cloth caps. They had a stiffened false front in the facing colour, displaying the Colonel's arms or in some cases the monarch's monogram, and a red unstiffened bag or stocking behind. Since the Royal Regiment was actually on the English establishment it comes as no surprise to find its grenadiers sporting white fronted cloth caps in 1684 and the Scots Guards too had cloth ones in the following year. By contrast there is a fair amount of evidence to show that Scots Grenadiers continued to wear furred caps until they were absorbed into the British Army after 1707.

The artillery certainly had furred caps in 1683 and presumably the grenadiers of the Scots Fusiliers had them too since they were so closely associated with the artillery. In 1688 the regiment, still at that time a normal infantry unit, was transferred on to the English establishment and appears to have become Fusiliers in about 1690. A red-faced officer's fusilier cap with King William's cypher on the front, presently in the Scottish United Services Museum, presumably belonged to an officer of the Scots Fusiliers.

   The grenadiers of the Earl of Argyle's Regiment had fur caps and it seems that the Earl of Angus's grenadiers also had them since they were supplied in 1691 with grenadier caps and grenadier cap badges. Since badges and cyphers were embroidered on cloth caps those issued to Angus's grenadiers must have been metal badges - perhaps a grenade device - for furred caps. The accounts for clothing supplied to the Earl of Lindsay's Regiment in 1694 merely speak of grenadier caps but as no facing colour is mentioned - unlike the drummers' caps issued at the same time - it may reasonably be concluded that these too were furred caps.

Immediately after the Restoration the personal equipment issued to each soldier was the same as during the Civil War. That is to say a shoulder belt or baldric of buff leather suspending a cheap sword, and for musketeers a collar of bandoliers slung over the other shoulder. Since militia muskets at least were supposed to take 16 balls to the pound of lead (the old *caliver* bore) 16 bandoliers or charges will have been suspended from each collar. At the end of the 1670s bayonets began to be issued, initially only to grenadiers and other men armed with firelocks (bayonets were not intended to replace pikes but to discourage soldiers from using their comparatively fragile firelocks as clubs - matchlocks were much more robust). In order to carry the bayonet it was necessary to replace the baldric with a waist belt or girdle carrying both sword and bayonet. Grenadiers also required a leather grenade bag which perforce necessitated the replacement of the collar of bandoliers (apart from being highly inconvenient for grenadiers it was slung over the same shoulder). In the English army grenadiers carried both cartridges and grenades in the same bag but the practice in the Scots army may have been different. There are references to cartouche boxes and to *patronashes* both holding cartridges. The first was the familiar cartridge box which eventually replaced the grenade bag and indeed was being used by musketeers of the Scots Guards as early as 1685 but the second may have been a slightly smaller version worn on the waistbelt, also used in the French and Dutch armies.

NOTES

A considerable amount of documentation exists regarding the problems which officers had in obtaining red cloth for coats in the face of protectionist pressure from the New Mills Cloth Manufactory. This can be found in the Register of the Privy Council of Scotland particularly for the years 1684 and 1688 (when they finally managed to persuade King James to ban the importation of cloth into Scotland for uniforms). For other references see the individual regiments concerned.

SCOTS GUARDS

Succession of Colonels:

George Livingston, 3rd Earl of Linlithgow	
Hon. James Douglas	13.6.1684
George Ramsay	1.9.1691
William Ker, Lord Jedburgh	25.4.1707

This regiment had its origin in a single company of foot commanded by John, Earl of Middleton, raised to garrison Edinburgh Castle after the Restoration. In 1662 however the first steps were taken to erect it into a regiment and its first action was the battle of Rullion Green in 1666. It again fought against the Covenanters at Bothwell Bridge in 1679 and after the Revolution it fought in Ireland, most notably at the Boyne before proceeding to Flanders. In Queen Anne's time the regiment served in Spain but not until after the Union.

A useful collection of references exists concerning the uniform of this regiment. In 1669 the King ordered that the regiment was to be dressed in red coats lined white, they might earlier have worn grey but this seems unlikely since the Royal Scots were wearing red lined with white at least two years earlier. In 1684 at Houndslow Camp red coats lined white, with white breeches and stockings were noted and in the same year Major James Murray obtained leave from the Privy Council to import a quantity of English cloth for the use of the regiment. Not all of the cloth was of the same quality and most of it was presumably intended for officers' uniforms. In all he was permitted to bring in 110 yards of scarlet cloth, 92 yards of scarlet serge, 6 yards of green cloth and 18 yards of "mazerine blew". Besides which 30 yards of flannel, colour unspecified, were also included. The purpose of the blue and green material is a mystery unless Murray was slipping in some cloth for his personal use. The scarlet cloth and serge is sufficient to make scarlet coats probably for the officers and sergeants. In 1702 250 ells of the "fynest light stone gray cloath" were ordered for the officers, presumably to make undress coats.

Although grenadiers had been introduced to the regiment as early as 1677 they were not formed into a separate company until 1682. An unreferenced description gives them white cloth caps with a lion's head and the royal cypher on the front but this sounds remarkably like the caps worn by the Royal Scots' grenadiers. It is possible therefore that, in the early years at least, furred caps were worn.

The white facings were changed to blue after the Union in 1707.

The grenadiers in 1682 were equipped with fusils, bayonets, patronashes (cartridge boxes worn on a waistbelt) and grenade bags. The rest of the regiment had to wait until 1686 to receive firelocks at which point there were 80 musketeers and 20 pikemen in each battalion company. The pikes were to completely disappear by Queen Anne's reign.

The first colours carried by the Scots Guards were quite unlike those normally carried by Scots units; "... red, with a saltire of St. Andrew's Cross, Argent in a field azure (ie in the canton), and a thistle crowned with this motto round the Thistle, Nemo me impune lacessit". Upon the accession of King James VII in 1685 however a more conventional style was adopted, being blue with a white saltire overall and the several captains distinguished by a roman numeral corresponding to their seniority placed in the upper quarter of the colour. As was usual with Scots regiments the Colonel's colour in accordance with continental practice was white. The Lieutenant Colonel's colour had no distinguishing marks whilst the Major's had a red pile wavy issuing from the canton.

Officers 1666 - Rullion Green

Colonel	George, Earl of Linlithgow
Lt. Col.	James Turner*
Major	William Hurry
Captain	Alexander Thomson
	Charles, Duke of Lennox
	John, Earl of Mar
	James Alexander
	William Borthwick
	Sir George Curror
	Adam Rutherford — ex. Royal Scots, coys. disbanded 1667
	Patrick Melville — ex. Royal Scots, coys. disbanded 1667
	James Leith — ex. Royal Scots, coys. disbanded 1667
	Earl of Lauderdale

*taken prisoner at the outset of the rebellion by the Covenanters but escaped just before the battle began.

Officers 1679 - Bothwell Bridge

Colonel	George, Earl of Linlithgow
Lt. Col.	Lord Ross
Major	Willam Borthwick
Captain	George, Lord Livingston
	Charles, Duke of Lennox
	James Alexander
	James Maitland
	Earl of Lauderdale
	James Carnegie of Finavon
	William Innes
	James Murray

1689

Colonel	Hon. James Douglas	- Colonel George Ramsay		1691
Lt. Col.	James Maitland	- Lt. Col. George McGill		1691
Major	George McGill	- Robert Murray	1691	
Captain	William Davidson	- George Macartney	1691	
	Patrick Ogleby	- Archibald Douglas	1690	
	William Hay	- Peter Ronald 1691		
	Robert Somerville	- John Mudie	1691	
	Earl of Carnwath	- John Stuart	1692	
	James Douglas (grenadiers)	- Thomas Hamilton		1691
	William Douglas			
	Robert Murray			
	Sir John Keith	- John Murray 1692		
	George Macartney	- John Hamilton	1691	
	Alexander Cunningham	- John Hamilton	1692	
	(John Innes)	- Thomas Hamilton		1690

1694 (two battalions)

Colonel	(Major General) George Ramsay		
Lt. Col.	George McGill		
Captain	Thomas Hamilton (grenadiers)		
	Archibald Douglas		
	Patrick (Peter) Ronald		
	John Hamilton		
	James Scott		
	Robert Muschet		
Major	Robert Murray	-	Lt. Col. 1695*
Captain	James Douglas (grenadiers)		
George Macartney		-	Major 1695
	John Stuart		
	John Murray		
	Thomas Scott		
	William Sharp		
	Henry Verrier		

* Earl of Dalhouse Lt. Col. 1696

Lawson, C.C.P. "A History of the Uniforms of the British Army" Vol. I pp. 61-3

Maj. Gen. Sir F. Maurice "The History of the Scots Guards" Vol. I (London 1934)

MERCURIUS PUBLICUS Sept. 18-25 1662 (early colours)

Minute Book of the Managers of the New Mills Cloth Manufactory pp. 328-9

Register of the Privy Council of Scotland (1684)   p. 381
(1685)   p. 166

Unless otherwise noted all officers listed here and under other regiments have been taken from Charles Dalton's "THE SCOTS ARMY 1661-1688" (London 1909 - reprinted London 1989) and "ENGLISH ARMY LISTS AND COMMISSION REGISTERS 1661-1714" (the latter includes regiments belonging to the Scottish Establishment from 1689 - 1707)

Succession of Colonels:

26. 1.1633	Sir John Hepburn
1636	George Hepburn
1637	Lord James Douglas
1645	Archibald Douglas, Earl of Angus
21.10.1655	Lord George Douglas, Earl of Dumbarton
31.12.1688	Frederick, Duke of Schomberg
5.3.1691	Sir Robert Douglas
1.8.1692	George Hamilton, Earl of Orkney

The regiment was formed in 1633 but spent the early part of its existence on the continent before being recalled by Charles II in 1662 and placed on the English establishment. In 1667 however it returned to France until 1678. Thereafter it served on the English establishment as the 1st Royal Regiment of Foot or Royal Scots, fighting at Tangier and Sedgemoor. A mutiny in May 1689 was expiated by good service in Flanders at Steinkirk and Landen and in Queen Anne's time at Blenheim, Ramillies, Oudenarde and Malplaquet. Although the regiment was never to serve in Scotland during the period covered an effort was made to ensure that it remained a Scottish unit as may be seen by this extract from a letter from King Charles to the Privy Council in September 1666:

"Whereas the Scottish regiment under the command of George, Lord Douglas, did, in obediance to our orders, come over readily and cheerfully to our service, wee are resolved to intertain and recruite the same although we think fitt to raise the greatest part of the recruits here in this kingdom (England) because of the leavyes now making in Scotland for our service there (a reference to the raising of Dalyell's Regiment) yet, seeing the regiment is a Scottish regiment, wee have thought fitt to raise for it two hundreth men in that our ancient kingdom of Scotland ..."

In Scotland however it was known in its early days as the "French regiment" and service with it was unpopular probably because it served in catholic France under catholic officers. By the end of the century though this prejudice had disappeared.

In 1667 red cloth with white lining material was sent to France for clothing the regiment and this uniform continued to be worn at least until the Union in 1707 when blue facings were adopted. Nathan Brooks in 1684 noted grey breeches, light grey stockings and, for the pikemen, white scarves. The grenadiers had white worsted loops edged blue and a white false front to their grenadier caps on which was embroidered a "lion's face proper crowned".

1666

Colonel	George, Lord Douglas
Lt. Col.	John Rattray
Major	Alexander Monro
Captain	Adam Tyree
	Archibald Douglas
	Robert Towers
	Patrick Monteith
	John Stuart
	Patrick Livingston
	Lord James Douglas
	Thomas Bannatyne
	James Douglas

1684

Colonel	George (Douglas) Earl of Dumbarton
Lt. Col.	Sir James Halket
Major	Archibald Douglas
Captain	Patrick Melville
	Robert Douglas
	Andrew Monro
	Robert Lawder
	Archibald Rollo
	Sir James Moray
	Robert Lundy
	Lord George Hamilton
	Charles Barclay
	James Moncrief
	Robert Hodges (grenadiers)
	Charles Moray
	John Ruthven
	John Carr
	James Forbes
	John White
	George Murray
	Lord James Murray

1685 (February)

Lt. Col.	Archibald Douglas
Major	Robert Douglas
Captain	Andrew Monro
	Robert Lawder
	Sir James Murray - Geo. Graeme 1686
	Lord George Hamilton
	James Moncrief
	Robert Hodges (grenadiers)
	Charles Barclay
	Sir Chas. Moray - John Johnson 1686
	John Ruthven
	John Carr - John Dufour 1686
	Thomas Forbes
	John White
	George Murray
	Lord James Murray
	Alexander Cunningham
	Murdo McKenzie
	Robert Halket
	Thomas Ogilvie

1687 (November)

Lt. Col.	Archibald Douglas*
Major	Sir Robert Douglas
Captain	Andrew Monro
	Robert Lawder
	Lord GeorgeHamilton
	James Moncrief
	Robert Hodges (grenadiers)*
	Charles Barclay
	John Ruthven
	Thomas Forbes
	John White
	George Murray
	Lord James Murray
	Alexander Cunningham
	Murdo McKenzie*
	Robert Helket
	Thomas Ogilvie
	John Johnston
	George Graeme
	Thomas Scott

*These companies and one other besides drawn off to form nucleus of a regiment which was later to become 16th Foot. Although initially led by Archibald Douglas it was taken over at the Revolution by Robert Hodges who led it with some distinction at Walcourt in 1689. He was eventually slain at Steinkirk in 1692. As might perhaps be expected the uniform of this new regiment was the same as the Royal Scots - red coats turned up with white.

Four additional companies were raised for the Royal Scots in September 1688 to replace those drawn off.

1688 (December)

Colonel	Duke of Schomberg	- Captain	Balthazar Guidet 1691	- William Kerr 1694	
Lt. Col.	(Sir Robert Douglas)*	- Lt. Col.	Andrew Monro 1691		
Major	(Andrew Monro)*	- Major	Thomas Forbes 1691		
Captain	James McCrakine	- Alexander Sanderson 1692		- James Lindsay 1695	
	Alexander Person				
	William Deanes				
	John Stirling	- Thomas Burgh 1692 (Stirling to 2nd Bn.grenadiers)			
	Robert Drury	- Archibald Hamilton 1696			
	Andrew Rutherford				
	George Stewart	- to Cunningham's Regt. 1689			
	Walter Murray				
	Lord George Hamilton	- Francis Stirling 1690			
	James Moncrief	- to Leven's Regt. 1689. Colonel of Foot 1693			
	Charles Barclay				
	Thomas Forbes	- Major 1691 : Lt. Col. 1692			
	John White	- Major 1692 : Lt. Col. 1694			
	Lord James Murray	- Colonel of Foot 1694			
	Alexander Cunningham				
	Robert Lawder				
	John Auchmouty (grenadiers)				
	Peter Wedderburn (grenadiers)				

* both temporarily suspended in December 1688 for refusing to acknowledge Schomberg as Colonel. Douglas eventually became Colonel and Monro Lieutenant Colonel but both were slain at Steinkirk in 1692

1702   Commissioned

Colonel	George, Earl of Orkney	-1 August 1692 (formerly Lord George Hamilton)
Lt. Col.	John White	31 August 1692
Major	Andrew Hamilton	10 June 1695 (commanded 2nd battalion)
Captain	Charles Barclay	1 June 1680
	Robert Kerr	1 October 1689
	Robert McKenzie	1 October 1689
	John Murray	1 January 1690
	Charles Cockburn	1 June 1692 (grenadiers)
	Thomas Burgh	1 August 1692
	James Hume	1 August 1695
	Alexander Irwin	2 August 1693
	James Lindsay	3 August 1695
	James Abercrombie	31 May 1701
	Lord Forbes	12 February 1702
(2nd Bn)	Thomas Bruce	1 October 1689
	John Bannerman	1 October 1689
	John Mowat	1 October 1689
	Charles Dundas	1 October 1689
	William Kerr	8 March 1694
	Peter Gordon	8 March 1694 (grenadiers)
	Adam Durham	5 August 1695
	Archibald Hamilton	18 January 1696
	Robert Hamilton	8 September 1692
	Lord Edward Murray	17 October 1701
	Thomas Kerr	12 February 1702

• Register of the Privy Council of Scotland (1666) p. 198
• Lawson, C.C.P. "A History of the Uniforms of the British Army" Vol. I p. 64

LIEUTENANT GENERAL THOMAS DALYELL'S REGIMENT
1666 - 1667

This regiment was raised at the outbreak of the war with the Dutch in 1666 around a nucleus of officers and men from the Scots Guards. It fought at Rullion Green in that year and was later employed on coastal defence duties before being disbanded on the 17th September 1667.

No details survive as to the clothing worn by this unit. It is possible that at this early date they may have worn grey, but red coats lined white seem much more likely particularly since the nucleus was drawn from the Guards.

Officers: August 1666

Colonel	Lt. Gen. Thomas Dalyell
Lt. Col.	Alexander, Earl of Kellie
Major	
Captain	John Hay
	Sir William Bannatyne
	Patrick Vaus

SIR WILLIAM LOCKHART'S REGIMENT 1672 - 1674

This regiment was raised in 1672 not by beat of drum but by conscripting fencibles. On the 4th March 1672 the Scots Privy Council agreed to a request from the King for 1,000 foot "which he conceaves may be more effectually done by proportioning them on the severall shyres and burghes of this kingdom then by beating of drums". The King agreed to arm and pay the soldiers thus raised - once they reached their embarkation points (Burntisland and Leith) - but the local authorities had to clothe them. Initially quartered in the south of England they soon acquired a rather unsavoury reputation - probably because the local authorites in time honoured manner had taken the opportunity to ship out all their rubbish - and indeed they even murdered a lieutenant when eventually embarked for France to fight the Dutch. Once over there they were disbanded in 1674 and the luckless conscripts drafted into the Duke of Monmouth's Royal English Regiment.

The Privy Council ordered that they were to be dressed in "blew coats lynned with whyte and have hattes". Usefully enough confirmation that this was actually provided comes from burgh records of Inverurie in Aberdeenshire where the Sheriff Depute received 50 merks for getting one Alexander Forfar to the dockside at Burntisland and kitting him out with a new blue coat lined with white and a hat "according to the act". No other provision of clothing appears to have been made and most of it must therefore have been the conscripts' ordinary civilian clothes with the blue coat thrown over. The choice of blue coats rather than red presumably reflects the fact that these soldiers were fencibles.

Officers: 1672

Colonel	Sir William Lockhart		
Lt. Col.	Patrick Menteith	-	Royal Scots 1666
Major	George Winrame		
Captain	John Dalyell		
	William Macdougall		
	James Douglas		
	John Sandilands	-	Royal Scots 1666
	James Lumsden		
	Sir Charles Halkett		
	James Menteith		
	Willam Arnott		
	David Bruce		
Captain	Lieutenant Paul Angier		

Register of the Privy Council of Scotland (1672) pp. 478-9
Davidson, J. "Inverurie and the Earldom of the Garioch" (1878)

MAJOR GENERAL SIR GEORGE MONRO'S REGIMENT 1674 - 1676

Ordered to be raised (800 strong) on the 25th August 1674 for service in Scotland, it saw no action and was disbanded on the 14th/15th January 1676. One hundred of the best men were retained in service and added to the Scots Guards.

No details are available as to the uniform worn by this corps.

Officers: 1674

Colonel	Sir George Monro	
Lt. Col.	William Fleming, Earl of Wigton	
Major	George Winrame	-ex. Lockhart
Captain	William Blair of Blair	
	Sir Patrick Ogilvy of Boyne	
	James Seton of Touch	
	John Riddell of Haining	
	Sir Robert Dalyell	

SCOTS FUSILIERS

Succession of Colonels:

Charles Erskine, 5th Earl of Mar	23.9.1678
Thomas Buchan	29. 7.1686
Francis Fergus O'Farrell	1.3.1689
Robert Mackay	13.11.1695
Archibald Row*	1.1.1697
Viscount Mordaunt	25. 8.1704
Sampson de Lalo**	26. 6.1706
Viscount Mordaunt	4. 9.1709

* slain at Blenheim
** slain at Malplaquet

This regiment had its origin in an independent company raised by the earl of Mar in 1677. Ordered to be trained as grenadiers it was also to be "instructed in all things belonging to the artillery, as gunnery, casting of hand grenades and fireworks". In September of 1678 however this company was expanded into a marching regiment of foot and appears to have lost its connection with the artillery, being equipped with 548 English muskets and as many bandoliers, and 272 pikes. Thus equipped it fought at Bothwell Bridge in 1679. A grenadier company was re-instated in 1682 and on the 18th of June 1686 Lieutenant Colonel Thomas Buchan obtained leave from the Privy Council to import from Holland 500 muskets with double locks - that is firelocks with a half-cock facility unlike the old English style firelocks which had to rely upon a dog or safety-catch. Drawn into England in 1688 it was sent to Flanders in April 1689 and remained there until the Peace of Ryswick, fighting at Walcourt, Steinkirk, Landen / Neerwinden and the taking of Namur. Under Queen Anne the regiment returned to Flanders and fought in all of Marlborough's victories.

When they became fusiliers is not clear. It may have been in 1686 when Buchan obtained these firelocks but the earliest recorded usage of the title appears to occur as late as 1691.

Early descriptions agree that the regiment wore "Red faced and lined the same colour, grey breeches and stockings". As is well known it was nicknamed "The Earl o' Mar's Greybreeks". Grey breeches were normal amongst Scots regiments in the 17th century but this probably goes back to the days of the independent company attached to the artillery in 1677. Both wore red coats lined red but Mar's men would have been easily distinguished from the gunners by their grey breeches since the artillery had red ones. In June 1684 the New Mills Cloth Manufactory was supplying material for the regiment's use, Galloway cloth for coats, Fingarinns for lining and so on, 18d being charged for making up each suit. A 1686 account in the same firm's books is very useful:

> "Deacon Kerr haveing presented his accomptt for makeing eight hundred and fourty suit of cloath for Marr's regiment, quhich cloath had five dozen of buttones, and the seames ironed more then the former cloaths he made, therfor allowes hime in contemplation therof and of other petty furnitur twenty shilling Scotts per suit".

Until the regiment became a fusilier one, hats will have been worn by most of the men. Although the original independent company and the grenadier company raised in 1682 presumably wore furred caps like the gunners, afterwards they will have worn cloth caps. A recent reconstruction of a sergeant of the regiment, based upon one of a set of lead figures from the Chelsea Bun Shop, gives the regiment a blue grenadier cap. However these figures do not appear to be a reliable source since they exhibit certain anomolies and while painted differently seem to have been cast from a common mould. With red facings one should expect to find a red fronted cap rather than a blue one and significantly just such a cap - an officer's one - does indeed exist in the Scottish United Services Museum, bearing King William's cypher.

The regiment's colours under James VII were blue with the usual white saltire. In the centre of the saltire was a blue roundel bearing a thistle and the motto NEMO ME IMPUNE LACESSIT. The seniority of the several companies was indicated by a roman numeral in the canton. In order to distinguish the colours from those carried by the Scots Guards and the Royal Scots a white pile wavy or flame issued from the centre into each quarter of the blue field.

• Lawson, C.C.P., "A History of the Uniforms of the British Army" Vol. I p. 64
• Minute Book of the Managers of the New Mills Cloth Manufactory pp. 67, 129
• Register of the Privy Council of Scotland
    (1682) p.470 (grenadier company)
    (1686) p. xxi (firelocks)

1688

Colonel	Thomas Buchan
Lt. Col.	John Balfour
Major	Thomas Douglas
Captain	Robert McKenzie
	Hew Montgomerie
	John Bell
	John Bruce
	Alexander Cairns
	John Wallace
	William Trotter
	Kenneth McKenzie
	James Middleton
	John Ramsay
	Robert Charteris (grenadiers)

4th May 1689

Colonel	Francis O'Farrell
Lt. Col.	Thomas Douglas
Major	
Captain	Hew Montgomery
	Robert McKenzie
	William Campbell (grenadiers)
	Alexander Straitton
	William Burnett
	William Sharp
	William White
	John Paterson
	John Kingsford
	James Conevan
	Robert Reid of Balnakettle

1702

Colonel	Archibald Row
Lt. Col.	John Dalyell
Major	William Campbell
Captain	Alexander Straitton
	John Crawford
	James Kygo
	Walter Sharp
	William Murray
	John Row
	Jacques de Montressor
	Henry Erskine
	James Campbell

October 1704

Colonel	John, Lord Mordaunt
Lt. Col.	Lindsay
Major	Walter Sharp - Lt. Col. Aug. 1706
Captain	John Dunbar
	John Patterson
	Alexander Fairly (grenadiers)
	Lewis Rivalt
	John Row
	James Montressor
	Henry Erskine
	James Campbell - Major Aug. 1706

LORD JAMES DOUGLAS' REGIMENT 1678 - 1679

This regiment was raised in 1678 for the war with France and taken on to the English establishment as was usually the case with units intended for service overseas. Douglas' Regiment however remained in England until its disbandment the following year at the close of hostilities.

No direct evidence exists as to the uniform worn by this regiment.

Officers: 1672

Colonel	Lord James Douglas	- Royal Scots 1666
Lt. Col.	Robert Towers	- Royal Scots 1666
Major	Patrick Lalis (La Lisle)	- Royal Scots 1666
Captain	James Hay	
	Charles Barclay	- Royal Scots 1680
	George Humes	
	John Preston	
	Alexander Urquhart	
	James Moncrief	- Royal Scots 1684
	William Mackay	
	Charles Murray	- Royal Scots 1684
	Walter Maxwell	
	James ffountaine	

COLONEL JOHN WAUCHOPE'S REGIMENT

Succession of Colonels:

11. 3.1688	John Wauchope
31.12.1688	Sir David Colyear
	(later Lord Portmore)
1704	John Dalrymple (later Earl of Stair)
1706	William Borthwick
1706	John Hepburn
1709	James Douglas

Raised by James VII in 1688 at French expense to provide employment for those officers and soldiers of the Scots Brigade who obeyed his call to leave the Dutch service. About a third of the officers subsequently remained loyal to James when William of Orange siezed the throne but the remainder stayed on and the regiment, commanded by Sir David Colyear, later Lord Portmore, served in Flanders. Since most of the officers had come from the Scots Brigade in the first place they got on well with their parent formation and in 1701 the regiment was to all intents and purposes given to the Dutch. After valiant service it was disbanded in Holland in 1704.

Unusually for a Scottish regiment at this time it was actually given yellow facings, presumably because it was actually formed in England and these were James VII's livery colours. In 1705 the battalion companies' hats were exchanged for fusilier caps; on the front of each were two lions rampant standing on either side of a rock with the motto FIRM (Dalrymple's arms) while the grenadiers' caps had a grenade and gun - presumably a cannon - embroidered in red and blue. It is not clear whether these badges were in additions to or instead of those appearing on the fusilier caps. At any rate hats for the battalion men re-appeared the following year when the regiment was taken over by William Borthwick, a professional soldier who had served in the Camerionians since 1689. After Borthwick came John Hepburn and some very ornate grenadier caps bearing his motto GRATUS ESTO and arms;

> *"Of the knot of the union made by the Britons (poss. the Union flag)*
> *And a sheaf of arrows the Hollanders arms*
> *And a lion as fierce as can be*
> *With a hand with a shable★*
> *And a horse at the amble*
> *And Guns and grenades in several parts stands*
> *And pictures of shables of steel*
> *And on the farrat of each grenadier's cap*
> *Are letters from the Colonel's name*
> *An I and an H wrought throu other twice*
> *John Hepburn for to expreme"*

★ sabre

One of Lord Portmore's colours - identified by a white unicorn device of the Colyears - was captured by the French, probably at Tongres.

• Ferguson, J., "The History of the Scots Brigade in Holland" Vol. III pp. 307-577

COLONEL JOHN WAUCHOPE'S/SIR DAVID COLYER'S REGIMENT: OFFICERS

1688   Original Unit

Colonel	John Wauchope	WAUCHOPE*	-Sir David Colyear 1688
Lt. Col.	Henry Graham	MACKAY	
Major	John Gordon	MACKAY	-Major John Dalyell 1689
Captain	Gavin Hamilton	BALFOUR	
	Aeneas Mackay	MACKAY	- to Mackay's 1689**
	Henry Balfour	BALFOUR	
	George Hamilton	WAUCHOPE	
	John Dalyell	WAUCHOPE	-Charles Bolburne 1689
	Sir John Johnston	ROYAL SCOTS (1686)	
	Thomas Brown		
	Francis Wauchope (grenadiers)		- James Colyear 1688
	Henry Cunningham		
	Henry Hatcher		

* Wauchope's Regiment in the Scots Brigade was taken over by Colonel George Ramsay in 1688.
** Lieutenant Colonel of Mackay's Regiment (Scots Brigade) in succession to James Mackay slain at Killiecrankie 1689.

1694

Colonel	Sir David Colyear	
Lt. Col.	James Colyear	
Major	Alexander Hamilton	- Major John Hepburn 1700
Captain	John Monalt (Mowat?)	
	John Hamilton	
	John Sinclair	
	Samuel Eyres	- William Yorke 1695
	James Bruce	- vice John Gordon 1692
	Peter Charles	- vice Charles Holburne 1693
	John Lewis du Bose	- vice Charles Carr 1693
	John Hepburn	- Major 1700
	Duncan Moor (grenadiers)	
	Arthur Innes	- Henry Ratrie 1695

1702

Colonel	David, Lord Portmore	
Lt. Col.	James Colyear	- Lt. Col. John Hepburn 1704
Major	John Hepburn	- Major John Hamilton 1704
Captain	John Monnet (Mowat?)	-
	John Hamilton	- Major 1704, Lt. Col. 1706 slain Malplaquet
	Arthur Innes	- James Paterson 1705
	Peter Charles	- Cornelius Kennedy 1705
	Theodore de St. Leger	- out of Regt. by 1704
	John Sinclair	- James Mongin 1704
	Henry Rattray	- out of Regt. by 1704
	William Ogilvie	- Major at Malplaquet - mortally wounded
	John Campbell	- Major 1706

THE EARL OF LEVEN'S REGIMENT
(THE KING'S OWN SCOTTISH BORDERERS)

Succession of Colonels:

19.	3.1689	David Melville, 3rd Earl of Leven
19.	3.1694	James Maitland
15.	4.1711	William Breton

Raised in Edinburgh in two hectic hours of the 19th of March 1689, largely from among the western Cameronians then thronging the city, it was first employed in blockading Edinburgh Castle. At Killicrankie however the regiment fought very bravely indeed, earning fulsome praise from General Mackay for their stand. Subsequently they served in Flanders fighting at Steinkirk and Landen but by the end of the war in garrison at Fort William and took no part in Marlborough's campaigns.

A colour taken by the French in the 1690s appears to have belonged to the regiment. It is white with a rose and a thistle in alternate corners. In the centre within a wreath of palm leaves is what is probably a representation of Edinburgh Castle and above it the motto NISI DOMINUS FRUSTRA, the motto of the city of Edinburgh.

The uniform worn by the regiment in its early days is a little obscure. By 1742 red coats with deep yellow facings were in use but this is by no means a reliable indicator of the dress worn in the 1690s. The Earl of Angus' Regiment, for example, had white facings in 1691 but, like Leven's, had yellow ones by 1742. On balance given the predominance of red coats lined white in the Scots Army prior to the Union it is most likely that Leven's were originally so clad.

The central device on this colour (left) is unclear and may not have been accurately recorded by the French artist who copied it. At first sight it might be a representation of the Bass Rock, taken from Maitland's arms, but on balance it is rather more likely to represent Edinburgh Castle for the city's motto appears above. A very similar colour (right) was carried by Alexander Stewart's Edinburgh Regiment which fought at Dunbar nearly 50 years before.

There are scattered references to cloth and coats having been provided by the New Mills Cloth Manufactory in or before June of 1689 and Mackay in his own account of the battle of Killicrankie relates how he "espyed a small heap of red coats ... a parte of the earl of Leven's regiment". Fresh clothing appears to have been supplied in late October of that year.

- Register of the Privy Council of Scotland (1689) p. 438
- Minute Book of the Managers of the New Mills Cloth Manufactory pp. 209, 211
- Lawson, C.C.P., "A History of the Uniforms of the British Army" Vol. I p. 144

EARL OF LEVEN'S REGIMENT: OFFICERS

1689

Colonel	David, Earl of Leven	- Colonel James Maitland 1694
Lt. Col.	William Arnot	- Lt. Col. Robert Keith 1693
Major	Robert Bruce	- died April 1700
		- Captain Lord Kilmaurs
Captain	Archibald Paton	- out of Regiment 1694 *
	Sir Robert Hamilton	- Major 1700
	Henry Verrier	- out of Regiment 1694 *
	William Hill	- out of Regiment 1694 *
	James Denholme	- Lord Elphinstone 1693
		- John de la Tour 1697
	John Fullartoun	- Lt. Col. to Lord Angus 1689*
	James Bruce	- Lord Strathnaver's Regiment 1693*
	James Lundie	- ( ) Brymer 1st August 1692
		- George Melville 1693
		- Archibald Hay 1695
	Charles Erskine	- William Maxwell 1st August 1692
	John Moncrief	- Christopher Pumphrey 1693

* these officers replaced by:-

Captain	William Gordon (grenadiers)
	John Cadour
	John Stuart
	Kenneth Lundie
	William Weir

1702

Colonel	James Maitland	
Lt. Col.	Robert Keith	
Lt. Col.	Robert Reid of Balnakettle	
Major	Sir Robert Hamilton	
Captain	William Gordon	
	John Cadour	
	William Maxwell	
	John Stuart	
	Christopher Pumphrey	
	William Weir	
	Archibald Hay	
	Patrick Ogilvie	- 2nd Lt. Col. 17 November 1704
	Lord Frazer	

THE EARL OF ANGUS' REGIMENT: THE CAMERONIANS

Succession of Colonels:

19.4.1689	James Douglas, Earl of Angus
1.8.1692	Andrew Monro
25.8.1693	James Ferguson
24.10.1705	William Borthwick
1.1.1706	John Dalrymple, 2nd Earl of Stair
24.8.1706	George Preston

Raised in the south-west of Scotland in 1689 many, though by no means all, of the original officers and men belonged to the presbyterian sect known as Cameronians from whence originated the regiment's nickname and ultimately its title. There were at first two battalions but partly as a result of desertion and indiscipline and partly as a result of the losses suffered in their heroic defence of Dunkeld against the highland army in 1689 they were reduced to a single battalion. The disbanded companies were chosen by lot and the men reduced into the remaining ones. Captain Andrew Monro was the senior surviving officer after Dunkeld - Angus himself not having been present, and his promotion to Colonel after Steinkirk in 1692 was well deserved. Unfortunately he was killed himself at Landen in the following year. In 1697 the regiment was transferred to the Dutch establishment but returned to the British army two years later. Under Marlborough they fought at Blenheim, Ramillies, Oudenarde and Malplaquet.

It is evident from the Register of the Privy Council of Scotland that no uniforms were received by the regiment prior to October 1689. A number of Edinburgh merchants having been contracted to provide 1200 red coats and 1200 hats, though not apparently any breeches or other clothing. That no lining colour was specified rather suggests the usual plain white one and this is confirmed by the Gerpines camp list for July 1691 which evidences red coats lined white for the Earl of Angus' Regiment.

On the 4th of July 1689 with the regiment about to march for the highlands an order was given by the Privy Council for it to be provided with the equipment then deficient, viz: 400 bandoliers, 400 swords and belts, 800 bayonets and 100 tents. It had earlier received 400 pikes, 500 firelocks and 40 halberds from the magazine at Stirling. Assuming it was up to its originally authorised strength of 1,200 men besides officers there were probably two musketeers for each pikeman.

Equipment issued to the grenadier company in 1691 included pie-coats, patronashes and belts, grenadier caps and grenadier's cap badges. The issue of cap badges confirms that at this time they must have been wearing the furred grenadier caps still apparently favoured by Scots regiments since any badges or devices appearing on cloth grenadier caps were either embroidered or painted.

- Lawson, C.C.P., "A History of the Uniforms of the British Army", Vol. I p. 65
- Register of the Privy Council of Scotland (1689) pp. 439, 487
- Dalton, C., "English Army Lists" Vol. III p. 171

THE EARL OF ANGUS' REGIMENT (CAMERONIANS): OFFICERS

1689

Colonel	James Earl of Angus	- slain at Steinkirk 1692
Lt. Col.	William Cleland	- slain at Dunkeld 1689
		- Lt. Col. John Fullartoun slain at Steinkirk
Major	James Henderson	- slain at Dunkeld 1689
		- Major Daniel Ker slain at Steinkirk
Captain	Daniel Ker of Kersland	- Major 1689
	George Monro	
	Roy Campbell	
	William Hay	- wounded at Dunkeld 1689 and slain at Landen
	Dhu Campbell	
	William Borthwick (grenadiers)	
	Robert Home	
	Graigmuir	- Coy. disbanded late 1689
	John Haldane	- Alexander Campbell 1691
	William Herries	- John Buchannan 1691
	James Lindsay	
	Ninian Steele	- wounded at Dunkeld and slain at Steinkirk
	James Gilchrist	- Coy. disbanded late 1689
	John Mathieson	- Coy. disbanded late 1689
	John Caldwell	- wounded at Dunkeld 1689
		- Henry Stuart 1691
	John Stephenson	- Coy. disbanded late 1689
	William Grieve	- Coy. disbanded late 1689

Replacement of Steinkirk casualities 1692

Colonel	Andrew Monro	- slain at Landen 1693
Lt. Col.	James Ferguson	- from Scots Brigade
Major	William Borthwick	
Captain	Hugh Fullartoun	- vice Lt. Col. John Fullartoun
	James Cranston	- vice Captain Ninian Steele
	George Murray	- vice Major Daniel Ker

Replacement of Landen casualties 1693

Colonel	James Ferguson	
Lt. Col.	Alexander Livingston	
Captain	John Blackadder	- vice Robert Tait
	Robert Monro	- vice John Campbell
	Andrew Monro	- vice William Hay

1694

Colonel	James Ferguson	
Lt. Col.	Alexander Livingston	
Major	William Borthwick	
Captain	James Lindsay (grenadiers)	- Alexander Cockle 1695
	Alexander Campbell	
	John Buchannan	- Thomas Turnbull 1695
		John Forrester 1695
	Henry Stuart	
	Hugh Fullartoun	

James Cranston
George Murray
John Blackadder
Alexander Monro
James Aikman

1702

Colonel	James Ferguson	
Lt. Col.	Alexander Livingston	- Lt. Col. James Cranston 25 Oct 1705
Major	William Borthwick	- Major John Blackadder 25 Oct1705
Captain	Alexander Campbell of Fonab	- (additional Coy. raised 1700)
	Henry Stuart	
	James Cranston (grenadiers)	- Lt. Col. 1705
	John Blackadder	- Major 1705
	Andrew Monro	
	James Aikman	
	William Drummond	
	John Dempster	
	Henry Borthwick	

Captaincies 1703 - 1706

William Hamilton	10 February 1703
John Lawson	1 May 1704
Wadham Spragg	25 June 1704
John Wilson	25 June 1704
Matthew Barnard	1 August 1706
Patrick Dickson	1 August 1706
Robert Ferguson	1 August 1706

MARQUIS OF ARGYLE'S REGIMENT 1689 - 1698

Commissioned on the 19th April 1689 and raised principally in the highlands, although the grenadier company was composed of veteran lowlanders from other units. Two companies of this regiment; Thomas Drummond's grenadier company and Campbell of Glenlyon's battalion company, took part in the notorious if sanctimoniously overblown "massacre" of Glencoe in 1692. Later that year the regiment went to Flanders and was in Dixemunde when the fortress was over-hastily surrendered. Exchanged in 1693 they took part in the assault upon the lines of d'Otignes in which battle the grenadier company was virtually wiped out. In 1694 the regiment was taken over by Argyle's son Lord Lorne and was disbanded in 1698 following the peace of Ryswick.

When Dixemunde surrendered the colours were said to have been torn from the staff to prevent theit being captured but one at least was taken and recorded in a book of French trophies, It has in the past been identified as a Scots Guard colour but only two Scots regiments were at Dixemunde - Argyle's and Graham's. The latter (formerly Ramsay's) belonged to the Scots Brigade whose colours appear to have been quite unlike that captured and their attribution to Argyle's is more likely. They are blue with a white saltire overall and thistle in each quarter.

The regiment's uniform has been reconstructed by John Prebble in "Glencoe" in some detail and only a summary is given here:-

Red coats were worn, faced yellow (must unusually), together with the customary grey breeches. Yellow stockings were issued and tartan waistcoats may have been worn. Battalion company men had blue bonnets with a boar's head and coronet badge worked on them. The grenadiers had fur caps.

On the 20th of May 200 firelocks were ordered for the regiment and patronashes were to be made in Glasgow to a pattern supplied by Auchinbreck. As he had been serving in the Scots Brigade these may have been of Dutch type. Whether the rest of the musketeers were equipped with firelocks or matchlocks does not appear and nor is it clear if the regiment included pikemen or whether like the Laird of Grant's Regiment they were all of them musketeers.

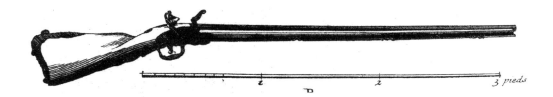

EARL OF ARGYLE'S REGIMENT - OFFICERS

1689
Colonel	Archibald, Earl of Argyle	
Lt. Col.	Sir Duncan Campbell of Auchinbreck	- Lt. Col. Robt. Jackson 1691
Major	Robert Duncanson	
Captain	Archibald McAuley of Ardincaple	
James Campbell of Ardkinglas		-Colin Campbell 1692
	Andrew Lamond	
	Archibald Campbell of Torrie	
	Archibald Campbell of Barbreck	
	Hector Bannatyne yr of Kearnes	
	Robert Campbell of Glenlyon	
	Thomas Drummond (grenadiers)	
	John Campbell of Airds	

1694
Colonel	John, Lord Lorne	
Lt. Col.	Robert Jackson	-Lt. Col. Patrick Home 1695 (briefly)
Major	Robert Duncanson	-Lt. Col. 1695 vice Home
Captain	Neil Campbell	-Major 1695
	Duncan Campbell	
	Thomas Drummond (grenadiers)	
	Colin Campbell snr -one of these replaced by Anthony Cador	

1697
	Colin Campbell jnr (	
	Robert Macauley	
	Alexander Campbell of Fonab	
	John Louis de la Bene	
	George Somerville	
	Robert Campbell of Glenlyon	-Robert Taylor 1696

JOHN, LORD BARGANY'S REGIMENT 1689

Commissioned on the 19th of April 1689 and subsequently reduced into Colonel Richard Cunningham's Regiment in January 1690.

No details are available as to clothing issued to the regiment although Lord Bargany afterwards complained that he had not been re-imbursed for monies expended thereon. Presumably the usual red coats lined white were worn.

Between the 25th April and 6th May 1689 280 muskets, 340 collars of bandoliers and no fewer than 360 pikes were issued by which it may be deduced that half of the regiment were pikemen, an unusually high proportion for this period. Muskets must have been in short supply.

Colonel	John, Lord Bargany
Lt. Col.	Patrick Graham
Major	Hamilton
Captain	William Thompson
Captain	William Hamilton

Register of the Privy Council of Scotland (1689) p. 55

ALEXANDER, LORD BLANTYRE'S REGIMENT 1689

Commissioned on the 19th of April 1689, raised in the south-west partly from amongst protestant refugees from Ulster and reduced into Colonel Richard Cunningham's Regiment in December 1689.

No details are available as to the uniform adopted by this regiment although the officers declared in a petition to the Privy Council in 1690 that they had raised and clothed their several companies at their own expense. Red coats lined white would seem likely.

In July 1689 Blantyre himself petitioned the Privy Council declaring that he had, according to his commission, levied 480 musketeers and 150 pikemen and requesting that the government supply him with swords and bayonets. In response 200 bayonets were ordered but whether this represented only the shortfall or whether only one musketeer in two of this regiment had a bayonet does not appear.

Colonel	Alexander, Lord Blantyre
Lt. Col.	William, Lord Forrester
Major	William Buchannan
Captain	Durhame
	Charles Swinton
	James Sleigh
	William Rowan
	Alexander Hume
	Alexander Young
	William Baillie
	Alexander Dunbar

Register of the Privy Council of Scotland(1689) p. 488

JOHN, EARL OF GLENCAIRN'S REGIMENT 1689 - 1691

Commissioned on 19th April 1689 and subsequently reduced into Colonel John Hill's Regiment in 1691.

No details are available as to clothing and equipment save for an allusion to patronashes being made in July 1689.

Colonel	John, Earl of Glencairn
Lt. Col.	John Houston of that ilk
Major	Burnett of Carlopps
Captain	Robert Dickson
	William Blair
	John Mackay
	Sir Alexander Livingston
	Nicol Buntein of Ardoch
	Gavin Hamilton
	James Hamilton

COLONEL LUDOVICK GRANT OF GRANT'S REGIMENT
1689 - 1690

Commissioned on 19th April 1689 and raised in the Inverness area. It remained in the area during the Jacobite campaign of 1689-1690. Part of the regiment garrisoned Urquhart Castle and a detachment was present at Cromdale. In late 1690 it was reduced into Colonel John Hill's Regiment.

The regiment was fully clothed by September 1689 having been furnished by several Edinburgh merchants. No details are available although the usual red coats lined white may be assumed. No mention however is made of hats and it is likely that bonnets were worn.

In December 1689 the Laird of Grant declared that he had purchased 600 bayonets, patronashes and belts made by a beltmaker named Robert Handisyde, and 500 firelocks. What type of firearm was issued to the remaining 100 musketeers is not known but it is clear that the regiment had no pikemen. It is possible that the patronashes referred to may have been the familiar cartridge box slung on a shoulder strap but a pouch attached to a waistbelt seems much more likely.

Colonel	Ludovick Grant of Grant
Lt. Col.	Patrick Grant (his brother)
Major	Hugh Mackay
Captain	Alexander Grant
	John Grant
	John Forbes yr of Culloden
	Laird of Burgiss
	George Gordon
	Robert Grant
	Robert Ross

Register of the Privy Council of Scotland (1689) pp. 228, 544

ALEXANDER, VISCOUNT KENMORE'S REGIMENT 1689 - 1691

Commissioned on the 19th April 1689, raised in the south-west partly from among protestant refugees from Ulster and ultimately reduced into Colonel John Hill's Regiment in 1691. It's most notable exploit was to take part in the battle of Killiecrankie where, completely isolated in the centre of Mackay's line it was one of the first regiments to run away. The fact that they put up no fight before taking their leave is emphasised by a tradition concerning the death of the regiment's Lieutenant Colonel, John Ferguson of Craigdarroch. He died it seems because his servant ran off with his horse and he in consequence could not run away fast enough on foot.

There are no details available as to the clothing worn by this regiment or indeed any evidence that they were clothed before the debacle at Killicrankie. There is however some correspondence relating to the equipment of the regiment in the Privy Council register. There were in all 450 bayonets required for the regiment so that there will have been only 150 out of the 600 men armed with pikes. In addition thirty patronashes were ordered for the corporals of the regiment although the ordinary musketeers were equipped with collars of bandoliers. Not surprisingly the regiment was in a somewhat parlous condition after Killiecrankie and in September 1689 Kenmore petitioned the Privy Council to let him have "what snapwarks, muskets, bandeleers they wanted" together with pikes and bayonets. In response the Privy Council ordered the regiment to be supplied with 200 muskets and 100 pikes.

Colonel	Alexander, Viscount Kenmore		
Lt. Col.	John Ferguson of Craigdarroch	-	slain at Killiecrankie
Major			
Captain	James Donaldson	-	prisoner at Killiecrankie
	James Gordon of Craichlair		
	Alexander Gordon		
	John McCulloch		
	Patrick Dunbar		
	Thomas Kennedy		
	William Gordon		

Register of the Privy Council of Scotland   (1689)pp. 542-3
                                              (1689)p. 152

EARL OF MAR'S REGIMENT 1689

Commissioned on the 19th of April 1689 and reduced into Cunningham's Regiment in December of that year. It may partly have been raised in the Stirling area where Mar had estates and partly in Aberdeenshire, for a petition by David Erskine of Dun, Mar's Lieutenant Colonel (Mar himself died shortly after the regiment was commissioned) stated that contracts for clothing the regiment had been placed with William Blackwood and Thomas Cussine in Aberdeen. Unfortunately he was not considerate enough to record what these uniforms, most of them issued by the end of August 1689, looked like. In the absence of any evidence to the contrary red coats lined white are most likely although the Scots Fusiliers, first raised by Mar in 1678, had red linings.

Colonel	Charles, Earl of Mar	
Lt. Col.	Sir David Erskine of Dun	
Major	Robert Forbes of Brux	- Coy. raised in Aberdeenshire?
Captains	Sir Thomas Nicholson	
	John Nicholson	
	George Preston	
	David Bruce	
	Alexander Hunter	
	Hugh Kennedy	
	John McKenzie	

Register of the Privy Council of Scotland (1689) p. 156

LORD STRATHNAVER'S REGIMENT 1689-1690

Commissioned on the 19th of April 1689 and disbanded in the following year this regiment was raised mainly in the far north and spent most of the highland war garrisoning Inverness and sending detachments upon punitive expeditions. At least two companies however were raised in Fife by Robert Lumsden of Innergellie, the son of a Scots general during the Civil War.

No information is available as to clothing or equipment although both appear to have been deficient.

Colonel	John, Lord Strathnaver
Lt. Col.	Robert, Lumsden of Innergellie
Major	George Wishart
Captain	Sleigh
	Salkeld
	Robert Monro of Foulis
	Adam Gordon of Dalfelly
	John Gordon of Embo
	George Gordon
	John Monro of Clynes

COLONEL RICHARD CUNNINGHAM'S REGIMENT 1690 - 1698

Commissioned on the 28th of December 1689 and to comprise 13 companies drawn from disbanded regiments. It was originally destined for service in Ireland but the continuing highland war kept them in Scotland first at Aberdeen and later at Braemar. Cunningham left the regiment in December 1690 to raise a dragoon regiment and command passed to John Buchan, an Aberdeenshire man.

Few of the original officers' names survive and the earliest complete list of company commanders dates from 1694.

1689 (Dec.)

Colonel	Richard Cunningham	
Lt. Col.	John Buchan	-ex. SCOTS BRIGADE Colonel Dec.1690
Lt. Col.	Sir Duncan Campbell	1691
Major	George Stewart	ex. ROYAL SCOTS

Captain	James Orrock	
	John Montgomery	
	Archibald Dunbar	Alexander Dunbar from Blantyre's?

1694

Colonel	John Buchan	
Lt. Col.	Meredith Gwyllims	
Major	Adam Cunningham	Captain John Wright 1696
Captain	William Reid	-Major 1696
	Sex Dalhern	
	James Orrock	
	William Baillie (grenadiers)	- ex. BLANTYRE
	Robert Hamilton	
	George Weir	-William Bruce 1695
	Johnston	-George Carse 1695
	William Baillie	-Thomas Hay 1695
	Archibald Dunbar	-James Colquhon 1695
		-Francis Forbes 1696

COLONEL JOHN HILL'S REGIMENT 1690 - 1698

Three regiments: Glencairn's, Grant's and Kenmore's, and Menzies of Weem's independent company were ordered on the 13th of November 1690 to be reduced into a regiment for Colonel John Hill to form the garrison of Inverlochy. His commission dated from the 2nd September but nothing was done about raising the regiment until November. It remained at Inverlochy/Fort William throughout its existence. A detachment was to have taken part in the "massacre" of Glencoe but was delayed by bad weather.

As to the regiment's clothing and equipment, 1,000 piecoats and a like number of pairs of stockings and shoes were ordered by the Privy Council. Since this was done before the regiment was actually formed it may confidently be supposed that these were the usual red coats lined white. On the 20th of October 1690 1,000 firelocks were ordered to be bough for the regiment.

Highland Independant Company

Colonel	John Hill	
Lt. Col.	James Hamilton	- Lt. Col. Robert Jackson (ex.ARGYLE) 1695
Major	John Forbes	- ex. GRANT Lt. Col. 1696 vice Jackson
Captain	Robert Hunter	
	Alexander Anderson (grenadiers)	- Major 1696 vice Forbes

James Cunningham   - Francis Farquhar 1695*
Anthony Wilkie
Neil McNeil
Lord Kilmaurs
James Menzies of Weem   - former Highland Independent Coy.

     * Farquhar took over the grenadier company in 1696 and Cunningham's old company   was then taken over by Captain Thomas Hamilton.

Register of the Privy Council of Scotland (1690) pp. 493, 523,565, 575

SIR JAMES MONCRIEF'S REGIMENT 1693 - 1714

Commissioned 1st February 1693 for service in Flanders. Taken over by Colonel George Hamilton 1st January 1694. Transferred to Dutch army 1697 temporarily returning to British service in 1699 before rejoining the Dutch army again in 1701. A colour appears to have been lost in the debacle at Denin in 1712 and the regiment was disbanded in Holland in 1714.

No direct evidence exists as to the uniform worn but the usual red coats lined white are likely. A colour taken at Denin is identified by a process of elimination. It is white with the royal arms in the centre and St. Andrew's cross in the canton.

1694

Colonel	George Hamilton	
Lt. Col.	Robert Lumsden	Lt. Col. Walter Macdonald Bowie 1695
Major	George Monro	Major John Douglas 1695
Captain	Alexander Stevenson	
	James Mosman (grenadiers)	
	Conyers	
	Patrick Erskine	
	William Crammond	
	Bourk	John Baillie 1695
		Edmund Harris 1697
	John Forbes	
	William Cunningham	
	James Muir	Archibald Pringle 1695
	Archibald Murray	Alexander Ross 1695

For some reason Dutch records are incomplete and only the following company commanders can be identified in Dutch service.

Colonel	George Hamilton	
Lt. Col.	Walter Macdonald Bowie	
Major	John Douglas	
Captain	John Crammond	James Crammond 1711
	John Findlay	Nicholas Balfour 1709
	John Balfour	

Lawson, C.C.P., "A History of the Uniforms of the British Army" Vol. I pp. 143-4

Commissioned 1st February 1693 for service in Flanders. Transferred to Dutch army 1697, temporarily returning to British service in 1699 before rejoining the Dutch army in 1701. John, Marquis of Lorne took over the regiment in 1704 and was then succeeded by John, Marquis of Tullibardine in 1706. Tullibardine was slain at Malplaquet in 1709 and command then passed to Colonel James Wood. One or possibly two colours were lost at Malplaquet and another at Bouchain on 19th October 1712. The regiment was disbanded in Holland in 1717.

As with Moncrief's Regiment no direct evidence exists as to the uniform worn. The colour lost at Bouchain is identified by a rather illiterate version of Wood's motto. It is white bearing in the centre a shield with the arms of England and Scotland side by side (not quarterly) within the garter. This is in turn surrounded by a gold cord knotted at intervals with thistles from which is suspended a St. Andrews medallion. The whole is surmounted by a crown and underneath is a blue ribbon bearing the motto MUNIT ET ORNAT. The presence of the union flag in the canton clearly dates the colour to after 1707 and it is presumably a replacement for one of those lost at Malplaquet. A colour recorded as taken there must have belonged to Tullibardine's since that was the only Scots regiment known to have lost a colour or colours. It is blue with a large gold thistle in the centre, crowned, and under it a white ribbon bearing the motto NEMO ME IMPUNE LACESSIT

Wood's Regiment (Dutch Service) 1712
White field, blue ribbons edged and lettered gold, gold thistles and roses edging garter

1694

Colonel	John, Lord Strathnaver	
Lt. Col.	Alexander Young	
Major	James Wood	-Lt. Col. by 1702
Captain	Charles Swinton	Major by 1702
	Robert Bruce	
	John Gordon	
	Samuel Fullartoun	-Lachlan Maclean 1697
	John Home	
	John Key	
	Thomas Drummond	
	John Brodie (grenadiers)	
	James Brown	
	John Jardine	

1703

Colonel	John, Lord Strathnaver	
Lt. Col.	James Wood	
Major	Charles Swinton	
Captain	Robert Bruce	
	John Jardine	
	John Home	
	John Brodie	-Major 1705
	John Gordon	
Captain	James Brown	
	Arthur Stewart	-John Young 1706
	Francis Farquhar	-Major December 1709
	David Graham	-slain at Malplaquet

Lawson, C.C.P., "A History of the Uniforms of the British Army" Vol. I pp. 143-4

N. Guerard, inuenit et fecit

LORD LINDSAY'S REGIMENT 1694 - 1698

This was one of three fencible regiments raised in 1694 and employed in home defence duties. To all intents and purposes they were embodied militia and this may account for the unusual uniforms worn by this regiment. Quartered in Glasgow and the west it was disbanded on the Peace of Ryswick.

A set of clothing bills in the Register Office in Edinburgh provides an unusually complete picture of the uniform. The soldiers wore coats of white Galloway cloth with forty-five loops on the grenadiers' coats. White breeches were also worn and red stockings. C.C.P. Lawson has suggested that the coats had red facings but there is no evidence of this and notwithstanding the red stockings the usual white linings seem more likely. Sergeants had red breeches and stone grey coats. They also had red cravats in place of the black and white ones issued to the men. By far the most interesting aspect of their uniform was the headgear:

> 748 Private centinels caps at 6s each;
> 26 finer caps for Sergeants, 10s each;
> 26 Drummers' caps faced with blue, at 6s each;
> Whereof one for the Drum-Major, to be finer than the rest, at10s;
> 56 grenadier caps at 8s each.

Both Lawson and Carman have concluded from this that the regiment wore fusilier caps (except the grenadiers of course). However it may be observed that while a facing colour is specified for the drummers' caps no mention is made of facings to the others. In view of this and bearing in mind that this was a fencible unit clothed in cheap undyed woollen coats it is rather more likely that the caps were Scots Blew Caps or bonnets, and that the grenadier caps, which also lacked facings were the furred ones which seem to have been favoured by the Scots.

Lieutenant Colonel James Hamilton		-ex. Hill
Major James Menzies*		-ex. Royal Scots
Captain	Robert Reid of Balnakettle	-ex. Scots Fusiliers.
	Thomas Young	-Lewis Lauder 1696
	William Bruce	-John Bellingham 1696
	Gairie	-Sir James Cockburn 1696
	Lindsay (grenadiers)	-Major 1697
		Francis Ross (grenadiers)

* Menzies murdered the Town Clerk of Glasgow in October 1694 and
was then killed himself while resisting arrest. Robert Reid of Balnakettle was appointed Major in his place and became Lieutenant Colonel of the regiment in December 1695.

Carman, W.Y., "British Uniforms" p. 49
Lawson, C.C.P., "History of the Uniforms of the British Army"Vol. I pp. 60-61

COLONEL ROBERT MACKAY'S REGIMENT 1694 - 1697

Fencible regiment commissioned on 1st January 1694 and employed in home defence duties. Taken over by Colonel George McGill 13th November 1695. Disbanded October 1697 - April 1698.

No details available as to clothing and equipment but may have been similar to Lord Lindsay's regiment.

Colonel	George McGill
Lt. Col.	John Dalyell
Major	Duncan McKenzie

Captain	Lord Reay
	Lord Edward Murray
	David Livingston
	Patrick Vaus
	Mark Ker
	Alexander Nisbet

g. HART '89

LORD JOHN MURRAY'S REGIMENT 1694 - 1697

Commissioned on 23rd April 1694 this fencible regiment was employed on coastal defence duties. It was disbanded between October 1697 and April 1698.

Other than the fact that it was described as being a strong regiment and well-clothed no details are available as to its clothing and equipment. It may however have worn white coats like Lord Lindsay's Regiment.

1694

Colonel	Lord John Murray (later Earl of Tullibardine)	
Lt. Col.	John Stirling	Lt. Col. William Hay 1694
Major	William Hay	Major Robert Pollock 1694

Captain	Hugh, Lord Lovat	
	Patrick Murray	
	Philip Anstruther	
	John (?) Bellingham	- Patrick Moncrief 1695
	James Drummond	
	Archibald Menzies of Culdares (grenadiers)	
	John Brodie of Brodie	
	William Grant	
	David Graham	
	Leonard Robertson of Straloch	

SIR WILLIAM DOUGLAS' REGIMENT 1695 - 1698

Very little appears to be known about this regiment and there are no details available as to the uniform worn.

Colonel	Sir William Douglas	
Lt. Col.	James Bruce	-Lt. Col. Scipio Hill 26 Nov 1696
Major	James Cunningham of Asket	
Captain	John Campbell	
	Charles Douglas	
	Thomas Turnbill	Samuel Livingstone 1696
	John Campbell	
	William Graham	
	Sheen	

THE EARL OF MAR'S REGIMENT 1702 - 1713

Raised in 1702 but remained in Scotland until 1708 when it went to Flanders. Taken over by Colonel Alexander Grant in 1706 it was disbanded in 1713.

No pre-1707 list of officers appears to be extant but the following officers serving in the regiment in 1709 had commissions dating from before 1707.

Colonel	Alexander Grant
Lt. Col.	
Major	William Clephane
Captain	John Buryard
	Alexander Cumming
	Charles Elphinstone
	Patrick Murray

LORD STRATHNAVER'S REGIMENT 1702 - 1713

Raised in 1702 but remained in Scotland until 1708 after which they served in Flanders until disbanded in 1713. Most of the officers appear to have come from the half-pay list.

Presumably the usual red coats lined white were worn.

Officers 16.9.1703

Colonel	William Lord Strathnaver	
Lt. Col.	William Lord Kilmaurs	ex. Hill
Major	(Lt. Col.) John Forbes	ex. Hill
Captain	(George) Winram	ex. Cunningham
	Alexander Straitton	ex. Scots Fusiliers
	Robert Urquhart	
	(Major) William Reid	ex. Cunningham
	Robert Sinclair	
	Tobias Smollet*	

* uncle of the famous writer

COLONEL GEORGE MACARTNEY'S REGIMENT 1704 - 1713

Macartney was a former Scots Guards officer and we may be fairly confident that his regiment was dressed in red coats lined white, the uniform of his old corps.

The regiment first served in Spain and fought at Almanza, returning to Britain it was re-organised and sent to Flanders in 1706.

Officers 29.6.1704

Colonel	George Macartney
Lt. Col.	Lord Mark Ker
Major	
Captain	Robert Nairn (grenadiers)
	David Wedderburn
	John Ramsay
	Dougall Campbell
	Charles Erskine
	Charles Cathcart
	Edward Cochran
	Lord Fincastle

NB. the names of the officers suggest that the regiment may initially have been raised principally in the Edinburgh area

LORD MARK KER'S REGIMENT 1706 - 1713

Raised in 1706 with the aid of officers from the half-pay list it went to Spain and fought at Almanza. Afterwards it joined the army in Flanders and was disbanded in 1713.

Officers 1.6.1706

Colonel	Lord Mark Ker	ex. Macartney
Lt. Col.	Harry Erskine	
Major	William Clephane	ex. Mar
Captain	Patrick Vaus Ker	ex. Mackay
	George Windram	ex. Strathnaver
	James Urquhart	
	John Nairn	
	Francis Ross	ex. Lindsay
	William Cleland Ker	
	Philip Lockhart Stewart	

The Scots Guards 1685

NOTE ON THE WINDSOR SKETCHES

Fig. A has a red coat lined red with a red waistcoat and breeches. Unlike C, however, he has red stockings and his buttons are on the right side of his coat. It is unlikely therefore that he is a soldier of Mackay's. Apparently a grenadier he wears a black cap, the details of which are unclear but which appears to be of Dutch pattern. It is just possible that he may belong to Balfour's Scots regiment but the cloth grenadier cap argues strongly for his belonging either to Tollemache's or Babbington's English regiments.

Fig. B has a grey coat faced red, red waistcoat and stockings. Tin buttons and a black hat laced white and turned up only at the right side. This is presumably a soldier of a Dutch line regiment (probably Birkenfeld).

Fig. C has a red coat faced red, red waistcoat and breeches and grey stockings. The pocket flaps on his coat are semi-circular. The buttons are tin and on the coat itself are on the left side. He wears a black hat laced white and turned up fore and aft. He is most probably a soldier of Mackay's Regiment; the description certainly fits.

Fig. D although there are some minor differences he clearly belongs to the same regiment as C. A grenadier, he wears a brown furred cap with a large red bag. It is noticeable that his buttons are on the left side.

Grant of Grant's Regiment 1689

Cavalry Trooper

Cameronian

Argyle's Regiment 1695

Portmore's Regiment (Dutch Service) 1703

Buchan's Regiment

Buchan's Regiment

40

Royal Scots

Royal Scots

Scots Guards 1686: Second Captain

Scots Guards 1686: Major

42

Scots Brigade 1712

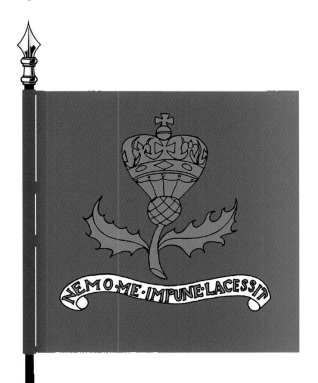

Tullibardine's Regiment (Dutch Service) 1709

43

Embroidered mitre cap of a Grenadier officer in a Scottish infantry regiment, about 1690. The front bears the joint cyphers of King William and Queen Mary between two thistles. The earliest example of military headress known to survive in Britain.

© National Museums of Scotland

THE SCOTS BRIGADE 1688 - 1697

Scots soldiers had been in the service of Holland since the 16th century and by 1688 comprised a brigade of three regiments. After a sticky patch during the Dutch Wars in the middle of the 17th century they had, since 1678, been regarded as being only on loan to the Dutch government, much as the Royal Scots were to the French, and could be recalled if required. This indeed occurred in 1685 during the Monmouth Rebellion but King James VII was disappointed when the Dutch for obvious reasons refused to again release the Scots Brigade into his service in 1688. There was a certain amount of cross traffic in officers between the Scots Brigade and the Scots standing regiments before 1688 but afterwards, with the Prince of Orange actually on the Scottish throne links between the two became very strong indeed. Brigadier General George Ramsay for example, the colonel of the third regiment became colonel of the Scots Guards in 1691 while a Scots Guards officer, Robert Murray, took over General Mackay's old regiment in 1697. Moreover officers originally commissioned into the Scots establishment who went into the Scots Brigade for a time retained their seniority.

The majority were raised by beat of drum by recruiting parties sent to Scotland for that purpose. It would even appear that in the 1670s recruiting parties for the Scots Brigade were active despite Scotland's being at war with Holland. The principal complaint against them being not that they were recruiting men for a hostile power but that they were in direct competition with recruiting parties for the Royal Scots, then in French service. It is noticeable too that the Dutch service seems to have been quite popular while the "French" recruiting officers experienced considerable difficulty - not least from local authorities - in raising men.

Whilst in Dutch service the three regiments each mustered ten companies of 55 men but once placed upon the English establishment by King William (but paid at the lower Scots rate while serving north of the border) they were brought up to thirteen companies in line with other British regiments. Upon the Scots Brigade's return to Dutch service at the end of 1697 the three additional companies in each regiment were disbanded.

King William also brought three English regiments with him from Holland. Two of them were retained on the English establishment in 1697 becoming the 5th and 6th Foot respectively whilst the third was disbanded. In order to replace them three Scots regiments were transferred to the Dutch establishment; Colonel James Fergusson's (Cameronians), Lord Strathnaver's and Colonel George Hamilton's. All three however were returned to the Scottish establishment in 1699 in return for Colonel Eppinger's Dutch dragoons but two years later in 1701 the Dutch again requested the services of three Scottish regiments. Strathnaver's and Hamilton's were again offered but this time the third was Lord Portmore's, raised ironically enough by James VII in 1688 to employ officers from the Scots Brigade. All three were ultimately disbanded in Holland in 1714 and 1717.

CLOTHING

As befitting British soldiers the three regiments were dressed in red, although the style of their clothing and equipment followed that of the Dutch army. Some sketches in the Windsor collection, wrongly identified by Lawson as typical British soldiers, show soldiers of the Dutch army at this time, two of them evidently members of General Mackay's Regiment (see appendix to this section for a discussion of the sketches).

The piecoats worn by the Dutch infantrymen had shorter sleeves than usual, exposing three or four inches of waistcoat sleeve. As a general rule waistcoat, breeches and sometimes stockings in Dutch regiments were of the facing colour and unlike British grenadiers Dutch ones did not wear "looped clothes".

Headgear for the battalion companies comprised the ubiquitous black felt hat bound around with white tape. Unlike Dutch line grenadiers, however, those belonging to the Scots Brigade had furred caps as were worn by regiments in the Scotish standing forces. Certainly this was the case in the early 1690s but in line with the British army stiffened cloth caps were introduced early in the 18th C. although ultimately they reverted to furred ones again.

At the beginning of the 18th C. curious white worsted tapes were sewn on to the sleeves of grenadiers and drummers' coats possibly to distinguish them from British regiments. It is possible that they may at first also have been given to the battalion company men as well for John Scot, a soldier in Lord Portmore's Regiment - not apparently a grenadier - records that in 1701 when the unit was transferred to the Dutch service new clothes with a shoulder knot were issued.

Officers and sergeants had coats of more conventional cut and although the Dutch service appears to have been much stricter in requiring officers to wear their regimentals rather than the rather casual undress favoured by officers at home there was some flexibility as to the colour of breeches and stockings. The officers and sergeants of Mackay's Regiment wore orange scarves but those of the other regiments jealously enjoyed the privilege of wearing crimson. Whether or not officers had the Scottish arms engraved upon their gorgets is not known but it seems very likely.

Personal equipment was basically similar to that worn by soldiers on the Scots establishment and is well illustrated in the Windsor sketches. There was a waistbelt supporting both plug-bayonet (later replaced of course by a socket one) and sword and a cartouche box slung on a broad strap over the left shoulder. The same equipment is worn by both musketeers and grenadiers in the Windsor sketches but most Dutch grenadiers had a small patronash or cartridge box on the waist belt and a leather grenade bag in place of the cartouche box. Unlike British soldiers a powder horn was also carried suspended from the waistbelt.

COLOURS

The oldest surviving colours of the Scots Brigade are laid up in St. Giles Cathedral in Edinburgh and date from the 18th C. In design they are quite simple being a union flag with the very prominent St. George's cross associated with the period and of course no red saltire for Ireland. In the centre is a crowned thistle proper and below it a royal blue ribbon bearing the old Scots motto NEMO ME IMPUNE LACESSIT.

A very similar colour however was taken by the French at Le Quesnoy in 1712, being blue with a white saltire overall and a gold thistle and crown in the centre with a red ribbon over it bearing the motto NEMO ME IMPOUNE LACESSIT. This colour must have been taken from either a regiment of the Scots Brigade or from one of the three auxiliary regiments since the British army had by this time withdrawn from the fighting. The close similarity which this colour bears to those in St. Giles clearly suggests that it belonged to the Scots Brigade.

A colour taken at Dixemunde in 1695 may possibly have belonged to the Scots Brigade since one of its regiments surrendered there but the style is quite unlike that discussed above and it is much more likely to have belonged to Argyle's the only other Scots regiment present.

THE SCOTS BRIGADE:
LIEUTENANT GENERAL HUGH MACKAY'S REGIMENT

Succession of Colonels:

1677	Hugh Mackay of Scourie
1. 8.1692	Aeneas Mackay
30. 5.1697	Robert Murray

Capable of tracing its origins back to 1574 this was the senior regiment of the Scots Brigade and not surprisingly was referred to as "The Old Regiment". Landing at Brixham with William of Orange a detachment of 25 men from the regiment (probably grenadiers) led by a Lieutenant Campbell beat off an attack by some Lifeguards under Sarsfield at Wincanton on 20th November 1688, the only fighting of the "Glorious Revolution". In 1689 the regiment served in Scotland most notably at Killiecrankie on the 27th of July where it suffered heavy losses. The Lieutenant Colonel, James Mackay, and at least three if not five of the company commanders died fighting at the head of a gallant band of "old pikemen" while others were captured.
 By 1691 the regiment was campaigning in Flanders again and Mackay was slain leading a hopeless attack at Steinkirk in 1692. Taken over by his nephew Aeneas Mackay, it susequently fought at Landen and Namur, suffering particularly heavy losses in the storming of the Terra Nova Bastion, being perforce led on by the Lieutenants and Ensigns.

A rough analysis of the officers given in Fergusson's study of the Scots Brigade suggests that the regiment was substantially recruited in the north of Scotland and probably included considerable numbers of highlanders.

In camp at Gerpines in July 1691 the regiment was recorded as wearing red coats turned up with red. This description fits a musketeer and grenadier in the Windsor sketches already alluded to. However, after the regiment was taken over by Robert Murray in 1697, white linings replaced the red.

THE SCOTS BRIGADE:
COLONEL BARTHOLOMEW BALFOUR'S REGIMENT

Succession of Colonels:

1684	Bartholomew (Barthold) Balfour
1689	George Lauder

Raised in Scotland in 1603 by the Earl of Buccleugh for the Dutch service it fought at Killiecrankie where, putting his back against a tree and refusing to accept quarter, Balfour was slain and command thus passed to his Lieutenant Colonel, George Lauder, who was to command the regiment until 1716. Unlike the other two regiments in the brigade it did not return to Flanders until 1692.

Judging by the names of its officers Balfour's Regiment would appear to have been principally recruited in the north-east and east of Scotland.

Other than the obvious fact of their wearing red coats there is no direct evidence as to the uniform worn by Balfour's Regiment during the period in question. Like Ramsey's it had yellow facings in the mid 18th C. but as the latter definitely had white facings at this time it would be most unwise to assume yellow facings in 1689. Coloured facings were at this time very rare in Scottish regiments. It is just possible that Balfour's, like Mackay's had red facings but on balance white facings seem much more likely.

THE SCOTS BRIGADE:
BRIGADIER GEORGE RAMSAY'S REGIMENT

Succession of Colonels:

1688	George Ramsay
1. 9.1691	Sir Charles Graham
31.10.1695	Walter Philip Colyear

Commanded in 1688 by Colonel John Wauchope this was the youngest of the three regiments, having been raised in 1675 by Sir Alexander Colyear. Wauchope obeyed James VII's summons to return home in 1688 and command of the regiment then passed to George Ramsay who led the Scots Brigade in Flanders. Ramsay was appointed Colonel of the Scots Guards in August 1691 and the regiment was taken over by Graham, but after the shameful surrender of Dixemunde Graham, one of the signatories, was cashiered in October 1695 and the regiment given to Walter Colyear who was to remain colonel until 1747!

The names of the officers suggest that for the most part it was recruited in southern Scotland.

In camp at Gerpines in July 1691 it ws described as wearing red coats turned up with white. Presumably therefore white waistcoats and breeches were worn also.

SCOTS BRIGADE: OFFICERS

Lieutenant General Hugh Mackay of Scourie's Regiment

1689		1692		1694	
Colonel	Hugh Mackay	Colonel	Hugh Mackay*	Colonel	Aeneas Mackay
Lt. Col.	James Mackay*	Lt. Col.	Aeneas Mackay	Lt. Col.	Walter Corbet*
Major	John Buchan	Major	Peter Watkins*	Major	JohnCunningham**
Captain	Walter Bowie	Captain	John MacDougall	Captain	Walter Bowie
	George Connock*		Hugh Macdonald		Frederick Lamy
	Peter Watkins		Walter Bowie		James Cunningham
	Charles Graham		Donald Mcleod		Robert Bruce
	Everard Halket		Frederick Lamy		John McDougall
	Alexander Lamy*		James Cunningham		Gerrard Cattenberg
	William Schaep		Robert Bruce		Hugh Mackay
	Robert Mackay (Grenadiers)				William McKenzie
	Angus Mackay*				Hugh Sutherland
					Donald Cameron

* slain at Killiecrankie	* slain at Steinkirk	*vice Hugh Macdonald
		** vice Donald Mcleod

Colonel Bartholomew Balfour's Regiment

	1689		1692		1694	
Colonel	Barth. Balfour*	Colonel	George Lauder	Colonel	GeorgeLauder	
Lt. Col.	George Lauder	Lt. Col.		Lt. Col.	Alexander Stuart	
Major	James Ferguson	Major	James Ferguson	Major	Donald Mcleod	
Captain	Walter Murray	Captain	Walter Murray	Captain	Walter Murray	
	Thomas Erskine*		Archibald Paton		Archibald Paton	
	Alex. Livingston		Walter Corbet		James Blair	
	William Nanning*		James Blair		George Preston	
	Barth. Balfour (jnr)		Andrew Bruce*		Robert Fleming	
	Alexander Gordon		Sir James Erskine		Sir John Keith	
					William Nicholson	
					William Yuill	
					Patrick Gordon	
* slain at Killiecrankie		* slain at Steinkirk			Robert Ferguson	

Brigadier George Ramsay's Regiment

	1689		1694	
Colonel	George Ramsay	Colonel	Sir Charles Graham	Cashiered for surrender
Lt. Col.	Geo. Sommerville (?)	Lt. Col	GeorgeSomerville	of Dixemunde
Major	William Murray	Major	William Murray	Major David Monro 1.7.1695
				Major David Nicholson
				20.6.1696
Captain	John Clerk*	Captain	William Halke	
	William Douglas*		William Graham	
	Walter Corbet		John Ramsay	
	John Gibson*		Joost Van Beest	
	William Miln*		George, Earl of Dalhousie	
			James Boyd	
* slain at Killiecrankie			Robert Muschet	-Robert Young 22.5.1694
			Simon Fraser	
			Christian William Lichterberg	
			James Alexander	

THE SCOTS BRIGADE:
NOTE ON SOURCES

This section has very largely been compiled from documents reprinted in Colonel James Fergusson's "Papers Illustrating the History of the Scots Brigade in the Service of the United Netherlands" published in three volumes by the Scottish History Society in 1898, 1899 and 1900. Some additional material on uniforms has been obtained from Vols. I & II of Lawson. Childs discussion of the Scots Brigade in "The Army of Charles II" and "The Army of James II and the Glorious Revolution" is most unsatisfactory largely because he appears unable to distinguish between the Scots Brigade and the English regiments in Dutch service and fails to appreciate that the Scots Brigade was composed of professional soldiers rather than religious refugees.

THE CAVALRY

THE SCOTS LIFEGUARDS

Succession of Colonels:

2.4.1661	James Livingston, 1st Earl of Newburgh
28.1.1671	John Murray, 1st Marquess of Atholl
26.10.1678	James Graham, 3rd Marquess of Montrose
1.5.1684	George Livingston, 4th Earl of Linlithgow
31.12.1688	James Douglas, 2nd Earl of Queensbury
29.9.1703	Archibald Campbell, 1st Duke of Argyle
11.1.1715	John Cochrane, 4th Earl of Dundonald

Two troops were raised in 1661 but the second of these was disbanded in 1663. A third troop was also raised in that year but was likewise disbanded in 1676. Although fighting against the Covenanters at Rullion Green in 1666 and Bothwell Bridge in 1679 this was very much a household unit employed in and around Edinburgh and prior to the Union did not attend upon the sovereign outside Scotland. A troop of Horse Grenadiers was added in 1702 but both were disbanded in 1746.

A very complete description exists of the uniform worn by the Lifeguards in 1698. The troop wore scarlet coats lined white with white cuffs, a blue waistcoat and breeches, gold lace on the hat and buttonholes both on the coat and waistcoat and a gold cord hatband. A red leather baldric covered (on the outside only) with blue velvet and edged with gold galloon and a similar carbine belt were worn. Ammunition for the carbine was carried in a blue velvet covered patronash worn on a small red waistbelt. Saddle housings and holster caps were blue edged with gold galloon and bearing the King's cypher and crown. Officers had red cuffs and gold lace on the seams of the coat. All metalwork, including sword hilts, was brass.

In 1700 there were some minor modifications although the white linings remained until the Union. Waistcoats became a fine light mixed grey cloth and the horse furniture was changed to scarlet. More importantly however troopers also received blue surtout coats lined white and the NCOs blue lined blue, both with cloth buttons. The officers receiving blue coats lined blue with white cuffs and gilt buttons. This was presumably an everyday uniform with the gold-laced scarlet coats being reserved for ceremonial occasions such as the Riding of Parliament.

Lawson, C.C.P., "A History of the Uniforms of the British Army" Vol. I pp. 90-1

LIEUTENANT GENERAL WILLIAM DRUMMOND'S REGIMENT OF HORSE 1666 - 1667

The first six troops of this regiment were raised in August 1666 and fought at Rullion Green. The others were raised between January and March 1667 and all were disbanded in September 1667.

No evidence appears to survive concerning their clothing although it was noted upon their disbanding that in a number of troops the men retained their pistols and holsters. It is more than likely that it this early date buff coats were worn.

Troop Commanders 1666

        Lieutenant General Thomas Dalyell *
        Lieutenant General William Drummond
        Duke of Hamilton
        Earl of Atholl
        Earl of Airlie
        Hon. Charles Maitland

* a volunteer riding in this troop was Major General Colin Pitscottie

Although nominally part of Drummond's Regiment the following additional troops raised in 1667 probably operated as independent troops and were largely disbanded in the areas from which they had been recruited. Since it was the troopers of those units who declined to sell their arms to the government it is possible that they were in fact fencibles.

Earl of Annandale	-raised in Annandale
Earl of Kincardine	-raised in Fife, Stirling and Clackmannan
Earl Marischal*	-raised in Aberdeenshire and Mearns
Earl of Dundee**	-raised in Forfarshire
Lord Drumlanrig	-raised in Dumfriesshire
Lord Carnegie	-raised in Forfarshire

*George Keith, 8th Earl Marischal (1661) served throughout the Civil War and   commanded regiments at Preston and Worcester

**John Scrymgeour, 1st Earl of Dundee, died 1668 without issue.

COLONEL JOHN GRAHAM OF CLAVERHOUSE'S HORSE
1682-1689

Formed on the 25th December 1682 from three independant Troops raised in 1678 and a fourth Troop raised early in 1683. On the 21st December 1685 a letter under the royal sign manual ordered it to be designated "His Majesty's Own Regiment of Horse". In practice it was afterwards referred to as the Royal (Scots) Regiment of Horse. By that time its establishment had been increased to seven Troops. In 1688 it marched into England to oppose William of Orange. Some of the troopers afterwards accompanied Claverhouse back to Scotland and fought at Killiecrankie but most of the regiment was disbanded in March 1689.

Originally the regiment would appear to have worn the ubiquitous red coats lined with white. In 1683 Claverhouse obtained leave from the Privy Council to import 150 ells of red cloth, 40 ells of white cloth and 550 dozen buttons - sufficient for 75 coats lined white with 88 buttons apiece. When making the regiment his own in 1685 James VII also ordered that the trumpeters and kettledrummers should wear his own livery and at the same time the coat linings were similarly changed to yellow. Lord Ross obtaining leave to import 120 ells of red cloth together with 160 ells of yellow baize and 20 ells of yellow serge. Lord Drumlanrig for his part obtained no fewer than 570 ells of scarlet cloth for cloaks, coats, saddle housing and holster caps and Airlie likewise imported 250 ells of red cloth for cloaks for his Troop. It does indeed appear to have been Claverhouse's Regiment which was refusing to buy cloth from the New Mills manufactory alleging that colour and quality were not acceptable. As most of the Scots army appears to have managed well enough it would seem likely that the cloth imported from England was not a common madder red but scarlet.

1683

Colonel John Graham of Claverhouse
Captain William, Lord Ross
        Adam Urquhart of Meldrum
        Earl of Balcarres

1688

Colonel	John Graham of Claverhouse	
Lt. Col.	Earl of Drumlanrig	- Lt. Col. Sir Charles Murray Nov.1688
Major	Sir Charles Murray	
Captain	Earl of Airlie	-William, Earl of Annandale Oct. 1688
	Sir William Wallace	-commanded remnant at Killiecrankie
	Earl of Balcarres	
	Lord William Douglas	

Terry, C.S "John Graham of Cleverhouse"	p346-9	
Register of the Privy Council of Scotland	(1683)	p172-3
	(1684)	pp102-3, 129-30, 355
	(1685)	p126

THE ROYAL (SCOTS) DRAGOONS

Succession of Colonels:

25.11.1681	Lieutenant General Thomas Dalyell
6.11.1685	Charles Murray, 1st Earl of Dunmore
31.12.1688	Sir Thomas Livingstone
7.4.1704	Lord John Hay
24.8.1706	John Dalrymple, 2nd Earl of Stair
21.4.1714	Sir David Colyear, 1st Earl of Portmore

This famous regiment had its origin in two independant companies of dragooners raised in Scotland in May 1678, being erected into a regiment in 1681. They fought at Drumclog and Bothwell Bridge in 1679 and afterwards took part in the great reviews at Houndslow under King James VII. Much inclined to Jacobitism the regiment made a number of abortive attempts to change sides during Viscount Dundee's uprising in 1689 but later gave good service under Sir Thomas Livingstone and even better service in Flanders with Marlborough's army.

Early references to the "Grey Dragoons" suggest that the regiment's nickname originally derived not from the colour of its horses but from its uniform. Stone grey coats were retained by the regiment both for officers and men until 1685 when it was transferred to England. This was at the insistence of General Dalyell presumably because until that time the regiment was chiefly engaged in counter-insurgency operations. Grey coats were far more useful to it in this role than bright red ones partly because they were generally less conspicuous but mainly because Dalyell had clearly appreciated the advantages of the soldiers engaged in counter-insurgency work being clothed in the same manner as those they were hunting.

In 1685 red coats and, as befitting a Royal regiment then on the English establishment, blue facings was adopted with tin buttons - replaced in 1692 by brass ones for some reason. Blue waistcoats and breeches also appear to have been in evidence.

The question of headgear is particularly interesting. Like most soldiers they had broad-brimmed black hats bound around with lace corresponding to their buttons and a hat band either of the same or of the facing colour. In addition, like other dragoons caps were also worn. English units normally sported furred caps like those worn by Scots grenadiers and the Scots Dragoons may have done likewise, there seems however to be a belief that Scots Blue Caps or bonnets were worn and this seems entirely feasible in view of their counter-insurgency role already alluded to. Wearing grey coats and blue bonnets they would have been virtually indistinguishable from the Covenanters they sought. In 1705 "buff shoulder belts were ordered besides new Grenadier caps to be made to the number of the Grenadiers" so presumably by this time the regiment included a Horse Grenadier Troop although these were shortly to go out of fashion. At what point the regiment won for itself the privilege of universally wearing grenadier caps is unclear although it had certainly been done before 1742.

Officers 1688		**1689**	
Colonel	Lord Charles Murray	Colonel	Sir Thomas Livingston
Lt. Col.	George Ratrie	Lt. Col.	Sir William Douglas
Major	William Douglas	Major	
Captain	John Strachan	Captain	Henry Balfour
	William Livingston of Kilsyth		John Hay
	Patrick Blair of Bogton		Sir William Douglas of Cavers
	Sir Adam Blair		

1694		**1695**	
Colonel	Sir Thomas Livingston	Colonel	Sir Thomas Livingston
Lt. Col.	John Hay	Lt. Col.	John Hay
Major		Major	Robert Preston
Captain	Andrew Agnew	Captain	Andrew Agnew
	William Murray		William Murray
	Robert Hunter (vice Cavers)		Robert Hunter
	David Crichton		David Crichton
	William Bennet of Grubett *		John Kerr - Tho. Young 1697
	Robert Preston *		

* additional troops

LORD CARDROSS'S DRAGOONS 1689 - 1690

Ordered to be raised on the 19th April 1689 this was one of a number of units hurriedly commissioned in the wake of the Revolution. Very largely composed of "Cameronian" volunteers it was principally employed in defending the Stirling area but was also involved in the bungled affair which led to the Earl of Angus' Regiment's epic defence of Dunkeld against the Highland Army. At the end of 1690 the regiment was disbanded, ostensibly to permit the formation of Cunningham's Dragoons although it was widely suspected that the government was more than a little wary of its fanatical leanings. Details of the clothing worn by Cardross's men are lacking but red coats lined white are possible. They were equipped with firelocks, swords and bayonets. Leatherwork was a dun buff colour and included a patronash - presumably on a waistbelt. Metalwork was of white iron.

Officers

Colonel Henry, Lord Cardross
Lt. Col. John Erskine

Major John Guthrie
Aide Major Robert Hunter
Captain Sir Alexander Home of Kerse
        John Home of Ninewells
        Walter Lockhart of Kirkton
        James Muir

Lt. Col. William Milne June 1689
- Lt. Col. Robert Jackson August 1689

later Scots Greys
Master of Cardross 1690

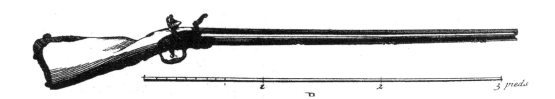

COLONEL RICHARD CUNNINGHAM'S DRAGOONS 1691 - 1714

Succession of Colonels:

30.12.1690	Richard Cunningham
1.10.1696	William Ker, Lord Jedburgh
28.4.1707	Patrick Home, Lord Polwarth

Formed at the beginning of 1691 from various previously unregimented troops of militia horse this regiment was sent to Ireland but after fighting at Aughrim went to Flanders. In Scotland after the Peace of Ryswick they returned briefly to Flanders in 1711 and were disbanded in 1714. Revived by King George I in the following year they eventually took precedence as the 7th Dragoons although they appear to have lost their Scottish character by the middle of the 18th century.

No details appear to be available as to the clothing worn by this unit prior to the red coats turned up with white noted in the 1742 clothing book. Carman however states that there is a regimental tradition that the white facings date back to the regiment's formation in 1691. Given the popularity of red coats lined with white in the Scots army in the 17th century, tradition may very well be right.

Officers 1692

Colonel	Richard Cunningham
Lt. Col.	William, Master of Forbes
Major	Archibald Paton
Captain	Robert Pollock
	George Douglas
	George Douglas

1695

Colonel	Richard Cunningham
Lt. Col.	William, Master of Forbes
Major	Patrick Home
Captain	John Johnston of Westerhall
	William Preston
	William Cunningham
	Stuart

LORD NEWBATTLE'S DRAGOONS 1691 - 1697

Like Cunningham's Regiment this unit had its origins in a number of Independent Troops of Militia Horse ordered to be raised on the 22nd April and 30th April 1689. These were:

Earl of Eglinton	r. Ayr and Renfrew
Earl of Annandale	r. Dumfries and Wigton
Lord Yester	r. Haddington and Berwick
Lord Newbattle	r. Roxburgh and Selkirk
Lord Rossr. Peebles, Linlithgow and Midlothian	
Lord Belhaven	r. Lanark, Stirling and Clackmannan
Lord Rollo	r. Forfar, Mearms and Aberdeenshire
Laird of Blair	r. Perthshire
Sir Charles Halket*	r. Fife and Kinross
Master of Forbes	r. Aberdeenshire (30th April)
Sir George Gordon of Edinglassie	r. Banffshire (30th April)
Captain William Benet of Grubbett	additional volunteer troop
Lord Polwarth	additional volunteer troop

    * given instead to Sir William Hope of Kirkliston 25th April 1689

The Laird of Blair's Troop was surprised and cut up in a skirmish at Perth early in the campaign but despite losing their Captain managed afterwards to soldier on. Belhaven's and Annandale's Troops - the latter led by his Lieutenant, William Lockhart of Cleghorn - both served somewhat ingloriously at Killiecrankie.

Combined into a regiment of dragooners in 1691 they were taken over by Lord Jedburgh in 1693 and finally in March 1697 by the Master of Forbes before being disbanded after the Peace of Ryswick.

At least two of the original independent troops wore red coats lined red as can be seen in this entry from the New Mills Minute Book:

22nd June 1689
"1260 Lykwayes the said George Home haveing mad bargone with the Earle of Annandale and Lord Ross for ther troupes viz :- ther coats lyned with Aberdaines fingarrins* dyed ride with eight dizen of buttons for threty five shillings and mad coat, payable ~ at delivery the other half between __ and the __ day of __ and approves of the same".

The Laird of Blair's trumpeter at least was described as wearing his master's livery and this was presumably also the case with the other troops.

As to equipment, pistols and carbines are mentioned in several documents relating to various Troops including the Master of Forbes' and Lord Rollo's. Whether the red coats lined red were adopted by other troops or continued after they were regimented does not appear but it is quite possible.

Minute Book of the Managers of the New Mills Cloth Manufactory p. 211
Register of the Privy Council of Scotland - various entries 1689-91

Officers 1692

Colonel   Lord Newbattle

Lt. Col.   Scipio Hill*
Major George Wishart

Captain   Lord Elphinstone
                Master of Polwarth*

-Lord Jedburgh 1693
-William, Master of Forbes 30.3.1697

-John Lockhart 1693

Hill's Troop had formerly been Captain William Benet of Grubbett's. Hill took over the Troop when the regiment was formed and at the end of August 1691 he complained to the Privy Council that most of the original troopers, unhappy at being demoted to dragooners (although in point of fact this was merely a money saving device for the regiment still served as Horse) had left taking their horses with them. This had put him to great expense and he was magnanimously in consequence awarded a month's pay. The Master of Polwarth, pleading the same case, obtained the same reward.

Rollo's Troop 1689

LORD CARMICHAEL'S / EARL OF HYNDFORD'S DRAGOONS
1694 - 1698 : 1702 - 1713

Very much kept in the family this rather obscure regiment served only in Scotland. It was first commissioned on the 29th of March 1694 and disbanded after the Peace of Ryswick in 1698. In 1702 however Carmichael who had in the meantime become Earl of Hyndford re-raised the regiment and was succeeded as Colonel in 1706 by his son James, Lord Carmichael. By 1713 when the regiment was finally disbanded he had in his turn become Earl of Hyndford. Had this unit ever actually seen action its rather singular succession of titles would doubtless have vastly confused French intelligence officers.

No details survive as to clothing but by this date red coats were more or less de rigeur. Lawson has a note that the equipment issued in 1694 included patronashes, firelocks and halberds - the latter presumably for the sergeants.

ARTILLERY AND OTHER UNREGIMENTED UNITS

The Scots Train of Artillery appears to have been dressed all in red. In 1662 the Gunner's coat was of fine scarlet cloth "laced with black velvet as the Yeomen of the Guard at London, embroidered with a thistle and crown and two cannons on the breast and one on the back and gunner's badges of silver".

Lawson, without giving a source, suggests that these gunners badges may have been a St. Andrew's cross worn either on the right breast or arm. This was of course very much a ceremonial uniform and working dress must have been much plainer.

In 1683 six suits of fine scarlet cloth lined with serge, with long silk loops, silver buttons, buff belts with silver buckles, buff gloves, furred caps laced with gold galloon, scarlet stockings and halberds were ordered. Again this is rather a ceremonial outfit but the clothing ordered for the under gunners probably gives a better idea of the everyday dress. They were to wear suits "so laced" with stockings, caps, buff belts with steel buckles rather than silver, together with patronashes, bayonets and grenade bags. Both the patronashes and the grenade bags bor the King's cypher on the flaps.

From this it is easy to reconstruct a uniform comprising a red coat and breeches, with the former presumably lined red, and red stockings. A furred grenadier cap with a red bag - laced with gold galloon for the officers - and for the under gunners at least grenadier equipment.

Little more can be added to this, Lieutenant General Drummond was authorised by the Privy Council in January 1685 to import 40 ells of scarlet cloth for the use of the artillery train - enough to make a suit for each of the twelve gunners and under gunners on the peacetime artillery establishment but otherwise no more details are available.

Garrison Companies

Independant Companies were maintained to man a number of fortresses, most notably Edinburgh, Blackness, Dumbarton, Stirling and the Bass Rock. In all cases they appear to have worn red coats. In 1685 the Privy Council authorised Captain Patrick Graham to import 300 ells of scarlet cloth from England for clothing the Edinburgh Guard - enough for coats and breeches although no mention is made of linings. The year before Major Andrew Whyte, the deputy Governor of the Castle, had obtained 220 ells of scarlet English cloth - enough for 110 coats. From the absence of any specific references one would expect to find white linings. On the 31st of August 1689 Henry Rollo of Woodside, the deputy Governor of Blackness Castle, petitioned the Privy Council for repayment of £46 16s which he had expended in replacing "ill clothing". After receiving confirmation that this money had indeed been expended on red cloth, linen (probably for lining the coats) and buttons the Privy Council grudgingly agreed.

The garrison of Dumbarton Castle in 1690 was ordered to be trained as grenadiers but whether their clothing was altered in conformity with this new role does not appear.

Highland Independant Companies

In 1667 Charles II commissioned the first independant highland companies, but even to a greater degree than the miniscule regular army they were intended to act as a gendarmerie, maintaining law and order in the highlands rather than serving as soldiers. Nevertheless they were noticeably better armed than most highlanders since firelocks and bayonets and even two stand of colours were issued to them. No clothing however was issued except during the infamous episode known as the "Highland Host" when shoes and "plaid" stockings were provided. Plaiding was a recognised width of cloth, not necessarily tartan material. As time went on some of these companies were attached to regular units presumably in an effort to exercise some control over them since far from upholding law and order their principal occupation seems very quickly to have become blackmail. Although most of these companies nevertheless remained in the highlands it is curious to note that the 25th Foot (formerly the Earl of Leven's Regiment) was still maintaining a highland company as late as the 1770s when it was stationed in Minorca. By that time it was clad as a light infantry company but did not wear highland dress.

The Company of Scotland

The Scottish planters who went to Darien, fought the Spaniards and died from Malaria, were organised on military lines and clothed accordingly. The soldiers were, sensibly enough, armed with firelocks and the manifests of the ship "Rising Sun" mention red coats. Some white coats also shipped may have been intended for officers' "undress".

Lawson, C.C.P., "A History of the Uniforms of the British Army" Vol. I p. 165 (artillery)

Register of the Privy Council of Scotland	(1685)	p. 99, 126-7	(artillery)
	(1684)	p. 513	(garrison)
	(1685)	p. 99	(garrison)
	(1689)	pp. 156-7	(garrison)
	(1690)	p. 306	(garrison)

Lawson, C.C.P., Op. Cit. p. 66 (highlanders)
Darien Shipping Papers (Scottish History Society) 1169   (Company of Scotland)

Note on Sources   As far as possible each unit has been separately sourced as necessary. All information of officers has, however, been obtained unless otherwise noted from Charles Dalton's Commission Registers of the British Army.

THE MILITIA

It was quite obvious in 1663 that the standing forces, effectively comprising at that time only the Lifeguard of Horse and the King's own regiment of foot (Scots Guards) were quite inadequate to undertake the defence of the country against foreign enemies or a serious insurrection. On the 23rd of September 1663 therefore Parliament offered to the King the services of a National Militia comprising 20,000 infantry and 2,000 cavalry "sufficiently armed and furnished with forty days provision" available for service anywhere in Scotland, England or Ireland. Nothing came of the proposal at the time and the so-called "Pentland Rising" was put down by regular troops, but in May 1668 the Privy Council received a letter and instructions from the King ordering the militia so offered to be established. Both documents are sufficiently clear to be inserted at this point in their entirety:-

"CHARLES R. *Right trusty and right weilbeloved cousine and councellour, right trusty and right weilbeloved cousines and councellours, right trusty and weilbeloved councellours and trusty and weilbeloved councellours, wee greit yow weill. Wee have formerly acquainted yow with our intention to setle a militia in that our auncient kingdome for the good of our service and preservation of peace ther, and now, after serious consideration, having thought of all particulars that occurred relating to it, wee doe hereby signifie unto yow our determinations. Wee doe think fit for the present to setle a militia only in the shyres which are sett doune in the inclosed list, and for the numbers of horse and foot to be stated in every shyre wee pitch upon the same that are sett doune in the 25 act of the thrid session of our late Parliament as most proper and competent, and for the distribution of them into regiments and troups it is our pleasur that, when the number of the foot of one shyre or of more shyres joyned together as they are distinctly exprest in the said act doe exceed 1100, they shall be divyded and constitut into two regiments, and when they are under that number they shall be put one regiment, and when the number of horss in the saids shyres exceed not 80 they shall all be but one troup, and when they are more then 80 they shall be tuo troupes. The troupes are not to be putt in regiments unlesse there be occasion to bring in any of them together and to putt the forces into a body, and, in that case, wee doe hereby authorise yow to putt them in regiments as yow shall think fitt and to appoynt commanders in chieff and uther officers necessary till our pleasur therein be knoune, and, as for the collonells and leivtennant colonells of foot and captaines of horse, wee have named them and shall very speedily send yow commissions to be delyvered to them, and doe hereby give the collonells power to choyse their majours to be approved by yow. And, because we conceave it be litle lesse difficult for yow then it is for us to condescend upon persons fitt (to) be captaines of foot and leivtennants and uther under officers of horse and foot, wee doe hereby appoynt yow in the choyse of such of them as have commissions to take the advyce of the collonells or commissioners of excyse and justices of peace in the respective shyres as yow think fitt; and, for the rest of the inferiour officers, wee doe authorise the captaines to name and appoynt them in their respective troupes and companyes to be approven by yow. And, because we judge it necessary there be in every shyre meit persons authorised for ordering and managing all particulars requisit for constituting and setling the militia according to our intention, wee hoehereby further declare it to be our will and pleasur that the commissioners that manage the excise and justices of the peace for the tyme being, together with the collonells, leivtennant collonells, majours and captaines who are not of their number, shall be trusted with that imployment in the respective shyres and borrowes, for the performance whereof wee doe hereby requyre and authorise yow to give them commissions, with fitt powers and order and instructions concerning all particulars competent to them from tyme to tyme as you shall sie cause. As to the numbers of companyes to be in each regiment of foot and of men in each company of foot and in the troupes where there are tuo troupes in our shyre or division, you shall either determin them yourselves or leave it to those commissioners as yow shall think fitt. Wee doe expect yow will quily transmitt to us the names of the majours and all other commissioners and we will send yow commissions for them, and it is our pleasur that all the commission officers take the Declaration. As for armes and amunition, wee have commanded the commissioners of our Thesaurary to furnish our oune magazin, and wee are weill pleased to hear that matter is a good forwardnes. It is now fitt tyme the countrey be provyded with armes lykwyse, at least for arming the militia, and wee doe therfore lay it upon yow to take care that armes be brought in to the countrey for that effect, and that the foot have none other fyre armes but musketts, and, when the armes come home from arming the militia in the severall shyres, yow shall take speciall care that none be sold but by your order. Yow shall also take security from sufficient men in every shyre that the armes for*

that shyre be not embezelled nor misapplyed to uthers then the militia, and yow shall only allow such a proportion of powder and match to each shyre as yow judge necessary for exercising, leaving to your care all uther particulars to this busines. And, if there be anything else to be ordered or done by us for perfecting what concerns the militia that we have here omitted, wee desyre yow to represent to us what occurres to yow thereupon that we may make knoune to yow our further pleasur. wee doe seriously charge yow to dispatch this business with all diligence, and doe expect ane exact accompt of your care herein speedily as being a matter wee have very much inour thoughtes and of high importance to our service, tranquility and weilfare of that our ancient kingdome. And so wee bid yow fareweell. Given at our court at Whythall, the 29 day of Apryle 1668, and of our reigne the 20 year. <u>Subscribitur</u> by his Majesties command.
LAUDERDALE

"Followes the list of the shyres and principall officers of the militia inclosed within his Majesties letter, dated 29 April, 1668 :- <u>Superscribitur</u>
CHARLES R.

Shyres	Collonells of foot	Leivtennent collonells	Captaines of horse
Roxburgh & Selkirk	(Duke of Buccleuch Thirlestane	Sir Francis Scot of	Duke of Buccleuch
	(Earl of Roxburgh	McDougall of McKerstoun	Lord Newbottle
Berwick	Earl of Home	Home of Plandergast	Home of Polwart
Edinburghshyre (Midlothian)	Earl of Lauderdale		Lord Ramsay
Haddington (East Lothian)	Earl of Tueidale or Lord Yester	Sir James Hay of Lunplum	Viscount Kingstoun
Linlithgow and Peebles	Earl of Wintoun	Murray of Blackbarony younger	Charles Maitland of Haltoun
Edinburgh, Leeth and Cannongat	Lord Provest of Edinburgh	Collonell James Hay	
Stirling and Clackmanan	Earl of Callandar or Lord Almont	Bucchannan of that ilk	Lord Cardross
Fyfe and Kinrose	(Earl of Rothes (Earl of Wemyss	Ardrose Sir James Lumsden younger	Earl of Kincardin Lord Newark
Perth	(Marquis of Montrose (Earl of Athole	Glenurchy Inchbreakie	Earl of Perth Earlof Tullibardine
Forfar	Lord Carnegy	James Carnegy of Bonimoon	(Earl of Airly (Earl of Dundy
Kincardin and Earl Marshall's part of Aberdein	Earl Marshall	George Keith, his brother	Viscount Arbuthnot
Argyle	Earl of Argyle		

<u>Subscribitur</u> C.R. By his Majesties command LAUDERDALE"

"Followes the memoriall for instructions to the commissioners for the militia in the severall shyres to be given by the Privy Councill, 29 Apryle 1668, inclosed within his Majesties letter":-

1. The <u>quorum</u> of the saids commissioners is to be a thrid part at leist of their number in every shyre.

2. After their first meiting to be appoynted by the Councill they are to meit upon their oune adjournments or advertisement from their conveener.

3. At their first meiting they are to chose their president or conveener.

4. The president to have power to call meitinges when he sees cause.

5. The conveener is to be chosen at the first meiting every new year, either by continowing the former or naming a new one.

6. They are to stent the numbers of horse and men upon the paroches, heretours and lyferenters in their respective shyres in the usuall maner.

7. To appoynt the number of men that shall be in each troup when ther is more then one in the shyre or division, and in each company of foot.

8. To state no company of foot less than 78 marching sojours at least.

9. To appoynt the number of companyes to be in every regiment in their respective bounds if the Councill doe it not.

10. To provyd colloures, drumes and cornets.

11. To sie the foot armed with picks and musketts at the expense of the heretours accotding to each mans proportion.

12. To allow of no fyre armes with snap workes, but that all be musketts.

13. To appoynt tuo thrids of each company to be musketeers and one piks.

14. To permitt no musketeer to have any match except when in service, or being allowed by the collonell who is to have it in his custody or send it to the Kings magazin in Edinburgh Castle.

15. To sie the horsmen conveniently mounted and armed with sword and pistolls at the heretours charges, and their horses listed with their colour and markes.

16. To cause list the names of the sojours, both foot and horse, with the names of every mans parent and duelling place.

17. To delyver lists of the sojours to ther captaines.

18. To change one sojour for another upon occaision with the captaines knowledge under whom he serves.

19. To choyse and list new sojours in the place of such as shall be removed by death or utherwayes and send his name to his captain.

20. To appoynt dayes of rendevous for mustering and exercising.

21. To rank the companyes in their regiments by consent or lot.

22. To cause visit the listed horses by some officer of the troup they belong to or other fitt persons once a quarter that new ones may be provyded and listed if neid be.

23. To judge and determin all questions and differences about disciplin, order, pretentions and all controversies among all officers and sojours belonging to their respective shyres in all military matters reconcile quarrells and punish these that faile in poynt of duty with imprisonment.

24. To punish with imprisonment or mulct or both such sojours as remove from their paroch totally to keep not their rendezvous without leave of one of their officers or their conveener in wryting.

25. To make use of no article of warr bot in so farr as concernes the ordinary rules of military duety, allanerly useing none other punishment but mulct and imprisonment and casheering of leivtennants and uther under officers when there is cause.

26. In all cases that are difficult and weighty to have recourse to the Lords of his Majesties Privy Councill.

27. To order and sie to the performance of all requisit poyntes of military duety when the regiments, companyes or troupes are at their rendezvous for mustering and excercise.

28. To take care that upon no pretext and officer or sojour be excempted from the authority of the law and ordinary judges in matters civill and criminall.

29. To condescend upon fitt persons to be captaines of foot and leivtennants of horse and foor upon vacancies as the Councill shall think fitt to appoynt, the collonells and superior officers being present, at least warned to the meeting.

30. To advertise the Lords of Councill with such new elections and send the names of the new officers to the Councill to be approven by them and transmitted to the King; as also when any superior officer dyes that new commissions may be obtained from his Majesty.

31. That the commissioners who, being warned or have notice of their respective meitinges, absent themselves without reasonable cause or leave of the conveener, be lyable to a fyne to be limited by the Councill.

The instructions actually sent out to the local commissioners although strictly in accordance with those given above were in some respects more detailed. Clause 10 of the Privy Council's instructions in particular related to the approved specifications and suppliers of the required weapons:-

"Yow are to sie the foot armed with pickes 15 foot long and muskets of one bore of sextein baalles to the pound at the expensses of the heretours according to each mans proportion, and these who are unprovyded of armes, as wee suppose most are, they may have good musketts at Leeth of the right bore from Alexander and Robert Milles, merchands in Linlithgow, for eight merks the piece, and under 24s Scotts the bandilieers, and the picks may be had in the countrey, good and cheap, made by Alexander Hay the Kings bowmaker in the Cannongate, and uthers, from whom yow are to provyde yourselves, being as cheap as anywhere else".

Even making allowances for the notorious corruption of the 17th century government it comes as a surprise to find such blatant advertisements in a set of official instructions (it is interesting though that the King's bowmaker had turned to the manufacture of pikes). Notwithstanding these blandishments most military supplies, especially of muskets, were obtained from Holland. Possibly of rather more interest to the individual militiaman was clause 22 which laid down that each foot soldier was to be paid six shillings Scots per day when mustered for duty and each horseman was to get eighteen shillings Scots.

A subsequent instruction from the Privy Council fixed the allowance of powder and match for each musketeer at a half pound and two pounds respectively each year for training purposes. No allowance of ball was made.

The stipulation that matchlocks wre to be used instead of firelocks was presumably intended to lessen the chances of the weapons being used illegitimately.

Ratified by an "ACT concerning the Militia" on 16th November 1669 there was nothing new in these instructions which were essentially unchanged since the Civil War, and even the suspect western shires were ordered to raise regiments. This is emphasised by the fact that the recruiting areas and the numbers of men for which each shire or sheriffdom was assessed were the same as in 1640, a point noted by Aberdeen Town Council;

7th April 1669
"The said day, the councell considering that the commissioners of this shyre for the militia had imposit vopn this burghe and freedome therof sexscoire men of ther companie in his Maiesties service thairanent; and withall considering that in anno 1640 the lyk number or therby was imposit wpon and put out by this burghe wpon the forsaid accompt ..."

Also reminiscent of the 1640s was the argument in Aberdeenshire over what part of the shire fell with the Earl Marischal's recruiting area and what part fell to the Earl of Kintore. The local authorities were quick to profess themselves to be sensible of their duty to put out their men but begged the Privy Council's direction as to where they should be assigned. This particular problem had led to endless squabbling in the 1640s but it was soon decided that the fencibles in all those parts of Aberdeenshire adjacent to the Mearns should go to the Earl Marischal whilst the remainder were to join with the Banffshire fencibles under the Earl of Kintore. The extent of those parts adjacent to the Mearns is unclear but they must have been quite substantial since only three of the Earl Marischal's companies were raised in the Mearns and he took the burgh of Aberdeen one for his own.

MILITIA UNIFORMS

As to the clothing worn by the militia references are tantalisingly brief but not entirely contradictory. The Privy Council issued no directions on this point nor even for that matter laid down any requirement that militiamen should be clothed at all. It does nonetheless seem to have been accepted by most if not all the local authorities that some clothing should be issued. The earliest reference to militia uniforms is in the minutes of Aberdeen Town Council. On the 6th of August 1669 the Dean of Guild was directed to provide 800 ells of red plaiding to make coats for the burgh's company. Plaiding was not tartan material but rather a narrow width wool as distinct from broadcloth and with a Scots ell amounting to only 37" the quantity ordered is about right for making up 120 knee length coats. No lining was mentioned but it was probably white in line with the rest of the army (the Aberdeen Militia were still wearing red in 1685).

The next reference, although in some ways less explicit, is even more interesting. On the 16th of October in that year the Earl of Lauderdale wrote to the King concerning some regiments of militia which he had inspected on his return to Scotland:

"In little more than threttie miles I have seen six regiments of foote in very good order & well armed, & five troups of hors; The Duke of Buccleuich's first, who was very well, both officers & sogers, & not a blew cap amongst them. His troup was very well, but the Lord Newbottles was the best mounted that ever I saw a Militia troup. The Earle of Roxbrough's regiment were good men & weell armed, but all blew caps, and the officers not to brag of. The Earle of Home's was every way well, & the Lord Yester's yet better. The militia regiment of this citty (Edinburgh) was very well. But if the militia regiment of this Shire (Midlothian) had not been mine, I wold say they looked best because all, both musket and pikemen were in blew coats lined with white, wch made a good shew".

Buccleugh's Regiment, with "not a blew cap amongst them" was presumably wearing hats and if these had been issued coats must have been issued as well, although Roxburgh's "all blew caps, & the officers not to brag of" sounds as though it had no uniform. As to the others, Home's, Yester's and the Edinburgh regiment, his silence suggests that they (and his own regiment) had hats since he would otherwise have commented adversely. His own regiment is clearly described as wearing blue coats lined white but the implication seems to be that it was alone in so dong. Nevertheless there is some evidence that blue coats were common amongst the militia or became so. When Sir William Lockhart's Regiment was levied in 1672 the local authorities were ordered to provide the recruits with blue coats lined white, not red ones, presumably because they were militiamen and not volunteers. A ballad about Bothwell Bridge in 1679 mentions Lothian militiamen "clad in their coats of blew". Since Lauderdale's Regiment had been left behind in Edinburgh those referred to may have been the Edinburgh and East Lothian regiments, both of which took part in the battle, but it would probably be unwise to interpret this particular reference so narrowly and it would perhaps be more accurate to take it as being a more general reference to the militia wearing blue than to its being the description of a particular regiment.

Once again it would most likely be fair to say that white facings will have been as universal amongst the militia as they were amongst the standing forces.

COLOURS

The colours, provided by the local authorities, appear in the first instance to have been the same as those carried during the civil war. That is a saltire covering the entire field, the tinctures of both being decided by the local commissioners, but on the 1st of August 1676 the Privy Council decided that this would have to stop:

"Item, that no foot colours be hereafter any uther then the Scottes collours, and that the collonells cullours be whyte, and that thereupon he may place what armes or motto he pleases, it being only for his owne company, and that the rest of the cullours have the name of the shyre upon them in great letters, and to be distinguished by bullets, crescents, starres or numbers as the collonell shall think fitt. Item, that the coronets or standarts of horse being provyded by the shyes themselves shall have the name of the shyre upon them and nothing else, and if the troup be out of the severall shyres, that the names of both shyres but putt on them conform to order of Parliament, and to be of what colour the captain of horse and the shyre shall aggrie to".

The former practice on the other hand may be seen in a petition by the Earl of Mar in 1677 on his succeeding to the command of the Stirling Militia;

"the said Earl of Marr on entering to his command found that the colours of the whole regiment were of the livery of the Earl of Callandar and not of the Scots colour, and besides they were wholly lacerated and torn, having been made use of since the first establishment, so he made new colours to the several companies of the regiment, in Scots colours, conform to the act of Council, and paid the price being £400 Scots 'by the attour the expences of the collours to his owin companie which he does not reckone, seeing he hes made them whyte conform to the act of Counsell and hes put his owne crest and motto upon them".

Lord Elphinstone in the same petition made a similar complaint in regard to the Stirling Militia horse standard which bore the livery and crest of the late Lord Cardross, his predecessor. His new standard was of the "Scots collours and motto conforme to the Councills act" and like Mar he received the cost of the new standard although it was not explained why he had waited five years to make the claim, Cardross having died and been replaced by him in 1672.

The resemblence to the colours carried during the Civil War is quite striking, red stars were used to distinguish three of the regiments at Preston in 1648 and another had numerals. Callander's livery incidentally was probably gold on black whilst Cardross's standard will have been very similar to that carried by his son's regiment of Dragoons - see Standing Regiments; Horse and Dragoons.

Another Militia Horse standard is illustrated by Lawson, being that of Lord Murray's Perthshire Troop. A white standard it bears his crest of a red lion rampart brandishing a falchion on a black rock with the inscription above; FOR ONE OF THE MILITIA TROUPS OF PERTH SHIRE 1684.

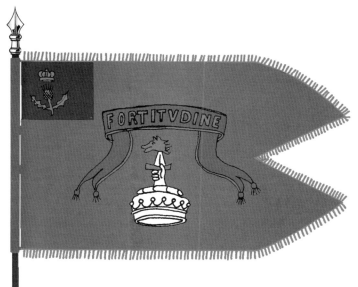

Cardross's Dragoons 1689 red silk, gold fringe, lettering and edging to red scroll, gold boars head and sword hilt, blue canton, gold thistle and crown

THE MILITIA IN ACTION: BOTHWELL BRIDGE

Continuing as it did the old fencible system the National Militia thus described was by English standards remarkably effective. Indeed as Dr Childs has commented it was actually possible to rely upon its marching towards the enemy rather than running away as the English militias tended to do. Militia service does not appear to have been unpopular and indeed was not without its advantages, militiamen in Aberdeen were exempted from taxes after 1673 to quote but one example. For the King a major advantage was the militia's willingness to be more than just a local defence force. In 1672 a marching regiment, Sir William Lockhart's Foot, was raised out of the militia and this may have inspired a proposed re-organisation of the militia in 1678. Earlier that year increasing unrest in the west had led to the rather heavy handed flag-showing exercise afterwards known as "The Highland Host". In actual fact nearly half of the host had been lowland militiamen and one of their more important tasks had been the disbanding of the unreliable Ayrshire and Clydesdale militias.

Although immensely unpopular the "Highland Host" appeared at first to have been a great success and at Lauderdale's suggestion the King decided to repeat the raising of Lockhart's Regiment on a larger scale. The Scots exchequer could not support a large standing army but yet more troops were seen to be necessary. The answer appeared to be a complete re-organisation of the militia into five regiments of foot each 1,000 strong, and five troops of horse each 100 strong. All the officers were to be professional soldiers, the regiments were to be trained for four days a month and slightly over half the cost was to be borne by the King, exclusive of the officers' salaries which were to be paid by the crown. The proposal, objectively, had much to recommend it but the "Highland Host" had reminded Lauderdale's enemies all too forcibly of their mortality and the Privy Council prevaricated long enough for the proposals to be forgotten. In the meantime rebellion had broken out in Fife and the West.

With the Re-Modelling of the militia a dead letter it was the existing National Militia which faced the crisis when it broke in June 1679, not a re-organised one as claimed by Childs.

With the understandable exception of the disarmed militia in the western shires all the regiments were ordered to be mobilised and assembled either at Stirling Bridge if raised "benorth" the Forth or Leith Links if raised in the southern shires. The orders having been given many of the old abuses at once manifested themselves. As in the early 1640s the command of most units had been given to local magnates without any real thought being given to their actual fitness for military command. In time of peace the Lord Provost of Edinburgh might have been the obvious choice to command the city militia regiment but when the time came for it to march westwards the Privy Council very sensibly re-assigned it (for the duration of the emergency) to a professional soldier, Lieutenant Colonel James Douglas. Others proved more willing, the Earl of Rothes was active in hastening the levying of his Fife regiment but as Lord Chancellor he was more urgently required in Edinburgh and soon recalled by the Privy Council. Colonels were not the only officers to be found wanting though, no fewer than four Captains in the Midlothian militia had to be replaced and three in the Berwickshire regiment. Nevertheless once they had shaken down the militia regiments formed the bulk of the government forces at Bothwell Bridge. No fewer than eight regiments appear to have been present (in contrast to no more than three regular regiments), most of them from shires to the south of the Forth:

Edinburgh Regiment	(Lieutenant Colonel James Douglas)
East Lothian Regiment	(Sir James Hay of Linplum)
Berwickshire Regiment	(Cockburn of Langton)
Perth - Earl of Atholl	(Major Murray)
Perth - Marquis of Montrose	(Lieutenant Colonel Patrick Graham)
Fife - Earl of Rothes	(Colonel Brymer)
Fife - Earl of Wemyss	(Earl of Wemyss)
Forfar Regiment	(Earl of Strathmore)

Other regiments were also involved though not actually engaged at Bothwell Bridge. Lauderdale's Midlothian Regiment remained behind to garrison Edinburgh, the Earl of Mar's Stirling Regiment together with the Linlithgow and Peebles Militia was needed to garrison Stirling and protect the Forth crossings - although Mar himself was ordered to join the army with his highlanders - and the Aberdeenshire Militia led by the Earl Marischal was marching hard to join the army when the news came that the rebels had been defeated.

Although there had been the odd hiccup this success enabled opposition to the New Modelling to continue until James VII succeeded to the throne in 1685. A firm believer in the benefits of a standing army he had no time for militias especially after the poor showning made by the English militia in the Monmouth rebellion. The Scots militia was therefore stood down. It was not disbanded, just ignored and by 1689 as useless as the English militia. During the Revolution it was rarely mobilised and only then for local defence - at which it was still effective. The militia horse was however a different matter.

Unlike the militia foot some attempt was made to keep the militia horse fairly efficient and on the 22nd of April 1689 nine Troops were ordered to be raised and others were added subsequently. These are fully discussed in the section dealing with Lord Newbattle's Horse.

APPENDIX ONE

Establishment for the pay of their Majesties' forces in Scotland, 1690

"Sic suprascribitur, WILLIAM R. Establishment for the pay of their Majesties standing forces of their Majesties ancient kingdome of Scotland, past under his Majestys royale hand at the court of Kensingtoune the first day of January 1690/91 and of their Majesties rigne the second year.

Tuo redgiments of dragoons quherof one comanded by
Richard Cunningham a collonell and the other by [blank]
and john, Lord Newbottle, as livtenant collonell and to each
of the said two redgiments as follows:

	Lib.	s.	d.
To collonell as collonell	..	:13:	8
To the livetenant collonell as such	..	: 7:	..
To the major as such	..	: 5:	..
To the quarter master	..	: 6:	..
Aid major	..	: 7:	..
Surgeon and mate	..	: 5:	..

Six troops belonging to each of the said two redgiments and
to each troop as followes:

	Lib.	s.	d.
To the captaine 8s. and three dragoons each at 1s. 4d., inde	..	:12:	..
Livetenant 5s. and one dragoone at 1s. 4d., inde	..	: 6:	4
Cornet 4s. and one dragoone at 1s. 4d. inde	..	: 5:	4
Tuo serjants, each at 2s. and 6d., inde	..	: 5:	..
Tuo corporalls, each at 2s. 8d., inde	..	: 3:	4
Tuo drummers, each at 1s. 8d., inde	..	: 3:	4
Fyfty dragoons, each at 1s. 4d., inde	3	: 6:	8
	5	: 2:	..

The redgiment of foott comanded by Collonell John Hill.

	Lib.	s.	d.
To the collonell as collonell	..	:12:	..
Livtenant collonell as such	..	: 7:	..
Major as such	..	: 5:	..
Minister	..	: 5:	..
Marischall	..	: 2:	..
Surgeon and his mate	..	: 5:	..
Aid major	..	: 4:	..
Smith and his servants	..	: 4:	..
A wright and his servants	..	: 4:	..
	2	: 8:	..

Tuelve companys belonging to the said redgiment
besyds the company of granadeers and to every company
as followeth:

	[Lib.	s.	d.]
To the captane	.. :	8:	..
Livetenant	.. :	4:	..
Ensigne	.. :	3:	..
Tuo serjants, each at 1s. 6d., inde	.. :	3:	..
Three corporalls, each at 1s., inde	.. :	3:	..
One drummer	.. :	1:	..
Seventy seven souldiers, each at 6d., inde	1 :	18:	6
	3 :	.. :	6

The company of granadeers belonging to the said redgiment.

To the captane	.. :	8:	..
The first livetenant	.. :	4:	..
The second livetenant	.. :	3:	..
Three serjants, each at 1s. 6d., inde	.. :	4:	6
Three corporalls, each at 1s., inde	.. :	3:	..
Tuo drummers, each at 1s., inde	.. :	2:	..
Seventy seven granadeers, each at 6d., inde	1 :	18:	6
	3 :	3:	..

The garrisone of Edinburgh Castell.

To the captaine	.. :	8:	..
To tuo livetennants, each at 4s., inde	.. :	8:	..
To the ensigne	.. :	3:	..
To four serjants, each at 1s. 6d.	.. :	6:	..
To six corporalls, each at 1s., inde	.. :	6:	..
To tuo drummers, each at 1s., inde	.. :	2:	..
To 154 souldiers, each at 6d., inde	3 :	17:	..
To the chaplane	.. :	2:	6
To the master gunner	.. :	2:	6
To fyve gunners, each at 1s. 6d., inde	.. :	7:	6
To the surgeon	.. :	2:	..
To the scriviner	.. :	2:	..
To the porter	.. :	1:	..
To the gunsmith quarterly 10 lib., inde per diem	.. :	2:	4
	6 :	9:	10

	Lib.	s.	d.
for coall and candle to that garrison yearly	40 :	..:	..

The garrisone of Stirling Castell.		[Lib.	s.	d]
To the captain as deputy governor		.. :	8:	..
To tuo livetennents, each at 1s., inde		.. :	8:	..
To the ensigne		.. :	3:	..
To four serjants, each other at 1s. 6d.		.. :	6:	..
To six corporalls, each at 1s., inde		.. :	6:	..
To tuo drumars. each at 1s.		.. :	2:	..
To 154 souldiers, each at 6d., inde		3 :	17:	..
To the scriviner		.. :	2:	..
Three gunners, each at 1s. 6d., inde		.. :	4:	6

	Lib. s. d.	5 : 16: 6
for coall and candle to that garrisone yearly	15: .. : ..	

To the garrisone of Dumbarton Castell.				
To the captaine		.. :	8:	..
Livetennent		.. :	4:	..
Ensigne		.. :	3:	..
Tuo serjants, each at 1s. 6d., inde		.. :	3:	..
Tuo corporalls at 1s., inde		.. :	2:	..
One gunner		.. :	1:	..
One scriviner		.. :	1:	..
The drummer		.. :	1:	..
Fourty tuo soldiers, each at 6d., inde		1:	1:	..

	Lib. s. d.	2: 5: ..
for coall and candle to that garrisone	15: ..: ..	

The garrisone of the Bass.				
To deputy governor		.. :	4:	..
One serjant		.. :	2:	..
One corporall		.. :	1:	4
One gunner		.. :	1:	2
Tuenty four souldiers, each at 8d., inde		.. :	16:	..

	Lib, s. d	1; 4: 6
for coall and candle to that garrisone yearly	15: ..: ..	
for boattmens wages yearly	20: ..: ..	

The garrisone of Blackness.				
To the deputy governor		.. :	4;	..
To the engine		.. :	2:	6
One serjant		.. :	1:	6
One drummer		.. :	1:	..
One corporall		.. :	1:	..
Thretty six souldiers, each at 6d., inde		.. :	18:	..

	1: 8: ..

	Lib.	s.	d.
for coall and candle to that garrisone yearly	8:	..	..

Fyve independent companyes, and to each
company as followes:

	[Lib.	s.	d.]
To the captain	..	8:	..
Livetennant	..	4:	..
Ensigne	..	3:	..
Three serjants, each at 1s. 6d., inde	..	4:	6
Three corporalls, each at 1s., inde	..	3:	..
Tuo drummers, each at 1s.	..	2:	..
Nynty seven souldiers, each at 6s., inde	2:	8:	6
	3:	13:	..

To the adjutant generall	..	8:	..
To the pay master and comissaries monthly	33:	6:	3
The phisician of the army	..	5:	6
To the artiliary, the generall not included, monthly	72:	9:	..

Tuo redgiments of foot quherof one comanded by Archbald,
Earle of Argyle, as collonell and the other by John Buchan
as collonell, and to each redgiment as followes:

To the collonell as collonell	..	12:	..
Livtenant collonell as such	..	7:	..
Major as such	..	5:	..
Aid major	..	4:	..
Quarter master	..	4:	..
Surgeon and his mate	..	5:	..
	1:	17:	..

Tuelve companyes belonging to each of these tuo
redgiments, and to each company as followes:

To the captaine	..	8:	..
The livetenent	..	4:	..
The ensigne	..	3:	..
Tuo serjants, each at 1s. 6d., inde	..	3:	..
Three corporalls, each 1s., inde	..	3:	..
Two drummers, each at 1s., inde	..	2:	..
Fyfty seven souldiers, each at 6d., inde	1:	8:	6
	2:	11:	6

To the muster master generall per diem	..	12:	..

By his Majesties comand. Sic subscribitur, MELVILL".

Scots Regular Infantry 1661 : 1707

Regiment	Raised	Altered	Coat	Linings	Butt	W/Coat	Breeches	Stockings	Head	Grenadiers	Notes
Scots Guards	1661	-	red	white	tin		white	white	hat	cloth caps	
Roual Regt.	1663	-	red	white	tin		grey	grey	hat	cloth caps	1st Foot (Royal Scots)
Dalywell	1666	-							-		disbanded 1667
Lockhart	1672	-	blue	white					hat	-	disbanded 1674
Monro	1674	-									disbanded 1676
Fusiliers	1677		red	red	brass		grey	grey	hat	fur caps	21st foot
		1690							fus. cap	cloth cap	
Douglas	1678	-	red	white			grey	grey	hat		disbanded 1679
Wauchope	1688	-	red	yellow					hat	cloth caps	disbanded 1717
Leven	1689	-	red	white	tin		grey		hat		25th Foot
Angus	1689	-	red	white	brass		grey		hat	fur caps	26th Foot (Cameronians)
Argyle	1689	-	red	yellow			grey	yellow	cap	fur caps	disbanded 1698
Bargany	1689		red	white							disbanded 1689
Blantyre	1689		red	white							disbanded 1689
Glencairn	1689										disbanded 1691
Grant	1689		red	white					cap		disbanded 1690
Kenmuir	1689										disbanded 1691
Mar	1689		red	red							disbanded 1689
Strathnaver	1689										disbanded 1690
Cunningham	1690		red	white							disbanded 1698
Hill	1690	-	red	white							disbanded 1698
Moncrief	1693	-	red	white							disbanded 1714
Strathnaver	1693	-	red	white							disbanded 1717
Mackay	1694		white								disbanded 1697
Lindsay	1694	-	white	white			white	red	cap	fur caps	disbanded 1697
sergeants	-	-	grey				red	red	cap	fur caps	
drummers	-	-	red	blue			blue	blue	-	-	drummers cap faced blue
Murray	1694		white								disbanded 1697
Douglas	1695										disbanded 1697
Mar	1702		red						hat		disbanded 1713
Strathnaver	1702		red	white					hat		disbanded 1713
Macartney	1704		red	white					hat		disbanded 1713
Ker	1706		red						hat		disbanded 1713
Mackay	1574		red	red	tin	red	red	grey	hat	fur caps	Scots Brigade
		1697	-	white					-	-	
Balfour	1603		red	white	tin	white	white		hat	fur caps	Scots Brigade
Ramsey	1675	red	white	tin	tin	white	white		hat	fur caps	Scots Brigade

Scots Regular Cavalry 1661 : 1707

Regiment	Raised	Altered	Coat	Linings	Butt	W/Coat	Breeches	Stockings	Head	Housings	Notes
Lifeguards	1661		red	white	brass	blue	blue		hat	blue	disbanded 1746
Claverhouse	1683		red	white	brass		buff		hat	red	disbanded 1689
		1685	-	yellow							
Dalywell	1681		grey						cap		2nd Dragoons (Scots Greys)
		1685	red	blue	tin		blue		hat		
Cardross	1689										disbanded 1690
Cunningham	1690		red	white							7th Dragoons
Newbattle	1691		red	red							disbanded 1667
Carmichael	1694										disbanded 1697
Hyndford	1702		red								disbanded 1713